BOOKS
SHOWN
READE
WRITIN
THE NUI

FINES C
INCUR
BE CHA

23.

22

26.

0

23.

03.

31.

2

GOLF
FOR WOMEN

Vivien Saunders

Photographs by
Michael Chittleborough

A & C Black · London

Published 1989 by A & C Black (Publishers) Ltd
35 Bedford Row, London WC1R 4JH

First published 1980 under the title
Successful Golf by
Charles Letts & Co Ltd, London

© Vivien Saunders 1980, 1989

ISBN 0 7136 5657 3

A CIP catalogue record for this book is
available from the British Library

Photoset by Rowland Phototypesetting Ltd,
Bury St Edmunds, Suffolk
Printed and bound in Great Britain by
Mackays of Chatham plc, Chatham, Kent

Contents

Introduction 6

1 Learning to understand the game 9
The mechanics of the game 9
The size of the ball 12
Two key points 13

2 The grip 14
Forming the grip 14
Adding the right hand 16
Alternative grips 21
Adjusting the grip 21
Tension in the grip 27
The key points 27

3 Setting up for success 28
The stance – front view 28
The ball position 30
The stance – side view 32
Distance from the ball 35
Direction 35

4 The basic golfswing 38
The simple swing 39

5 Developing the backswing 42
A simple backswing 43
The shoulder turn 47
The leg action 49
The hand action 49
The club position 52

6 Swinging through the ball 53
The arm action 60
Putting the two together 64
Balance 64

7 From short irons to driver 65
The short irons 65
Long irons 69
Long irons – a second approach 70
The fairway woods 70
The driver 71
Problems with driving 75

8 Ironing out faults 76
Correcting a faulty shot 77
Starting the ball on-target 78
The shot which starts left 79
The shot which starts right 80
Shots which curve to the left – the hook 81
Shots which curve to the right 86
Added problems for the slicer 89
Producing a solid contact 89
Topping the ball 92
Skied drives 93

9 The art of putting 94
Putting grips 94
The stance 95
Developing a good stroke 96
Choosing the right line 98
Good long putting 99

10 Short game techniques 100
Basic chipping 100
More advanced chipping 104
The up-and-over pitch 106
Adding height to the pitch 110
The long pitch 111

11 Better bunker play 114
The basic splash shot 114
Opening up in bunkers 117
Judging distance 122
The buried ball 123
Playing from hard sand 125
The downhill bunker shot 125
Fairway bunker shots 128

12 Shotmaking and situation golf 129
Recovering from thick rough 129
Chipping to a banked green 130
Playing into a bank 130
Punching a ball low 131
Producing extra height 131
Playing from sidehill lies 132
A long downhill shot 134
A short, downhill pitch 135
Playing from an uphill lie 135
Playing into the wind 136
Playing the tee shots 137
Deciding when to gamble 138
Short pitching from the rough 138

13 Ten keys to better golf 139
Swinging through the ball 139
Balance – the key to consistency 139
Visualising every shot 140
Think of the contact with the ball 140
Relaxation 141
Hit every shot for itself 141
Think of speed, not force 141
The swing as two movements 142
Watching the ball through impact 142
Back to basics 143

Index 144

Introduction

The popularity of the game of golf has grown very substantially over the past decade. The growth is partly due to greater television exposure and partly due to the attraction and glamour associated with stars such as Palmer, Nicklaus, Player and in Europe, Tony Jacklin and Seve Ballesteros. But perhaps the real reason for increased participation in the sport is the changing social and economic climate. We all enjoy more leisure time; we have more money to spend on leisure pursuits and this need is gradually being met by increased facilities and opportunities for participation. Commercial concerns have entered the golf market by building golf courses as profit-making ventures. They want the public to play, for the public is prepared to pay. Local government and sporting authorities have felt obliged to provide facilities for would-be golfers, catering for the increased leisure time and rising standard of living. Golf in much of the world is now a game for the general public to enjoy. Its previous mystique, with its incomprehensible jargon and image of be-tweeded upper class participants has dwindled – or is, at least, dwindling. It is gradually becoming a game which is open to all to play or to watch.

Golf, if one vigorously defends its merits as I do, is *the* game which offers virtually everything for the sports enthusiast – or even the not so enthusiastic. It is a game which can be played from the age of eight to eighty and even beyond. It is one of the few games where the champion can play with the novice and yet it is still enjoyable for both since the handicap system overcomes the differences. The delight is that you are not dependent on the opponent's shots for playing your own. The real challenge is your own shot and trying to tame the golf course. From the shotmaking point of view the opponent is almost incidental. You can play the game alone: the challenge is just as great.

It is a sport which requires just the right combination of ability, strength, timing and finesse. Very largely it is a question of technique and style, patience and concentration. Obviously golf, like any sport, is physically exacting for the real champion. But you can still play an excellent game in middle age or old age and without being a real athlete.

Part of the charm of the game is that it is so devastatingly hard for the beginner. And yet every session is highlighted by the odd shot of brilliance convincing you – or really deceiving you – that mastery of the game is not so far away. For the top class players the attraction of the sport is its unrelenting demand for perfection. The merest inaccuracy results in a less than perfect shot and generally a lost stroke. A moment's loss of concentration is almost always punished. There are no second chances – no second services. So it is a humbling, tantalising game.

But the real magic of golf is the exhilaration in simply being on many of the world's top courses. Even for the non-golfer, the pines and heather of Sunningdale or the views from Turnberry have an aura about them. Golf courses on the whole are scenic and well worth the walk even if the ball and game are fairly incidental. Each course is totally different from every other. The marvellous thing for the spectator is that you can often get within a matter of feet of the participant. You can watch and marvel from the scene of the action. And you can often play on the scenes of great championships yourself. The budding tennis player cannot hope to play on the Centre Court at Wimbledon; the footballer is not likely to sample the turf at Wembley. But the golfers can play at St Andrews or Sunningdale, drive from the tee Nicklaus drove from, use the same locker room, drink in the same bar and dream of playing the same game!

So golf, I suppose, has everything – or virtually everything – you could want from a sport. It is sociable; in which other sport can you carry on a running conversation with opponents, partners or spectators? It is humorous, serious, competitive, relaxing; it is what *you* want it to be. But above all, it is a sport very few ever really master!

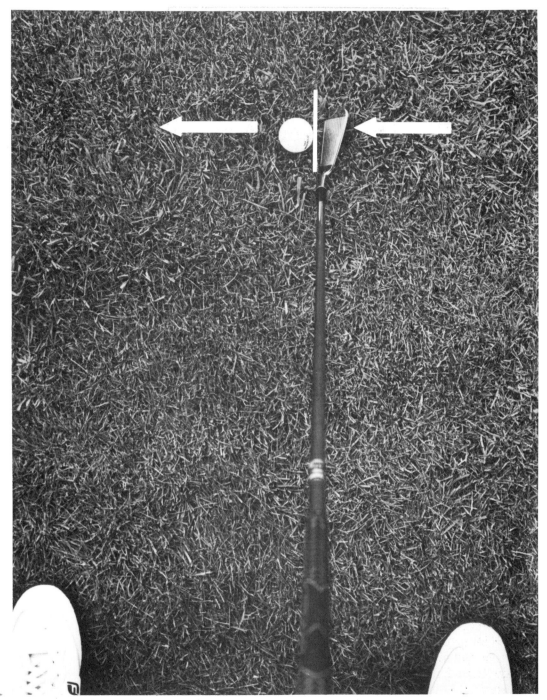

Fig. 1   The square contact — the clubface and swing are directed to the target

1 Learning to understand the game

One of the basic problems which arises in teaching golf is that pupils very often simply do not understand the fundamentals of the game. By this, I mean that they really do not appreciate sufficiently the way in which the club strikes the ball and how the corresponding shots are produced. Golf is not a simple game by any means. In many ways it is far more complex than the majority of ball games, and, for this reason, it is vital for pupils to grasp certain fundamentals before they can really hope to have any success as a golfer.

The mechanics of the game

The first area in which there is often complete lack of understanding is in the actual mechanics of the club and ball. Golf is unlike the majority of ball games in that a golf ball does not easily fly in a straight line. In most ball games the ball will fly relatively straight, and the skilled player has to work at and develop her method of producing sidespin on the ball as and when required. With golf, quite the opposite is true. The ball readily takes up both backspin and sidespin and the problem is largely one of minimising sidespin to produce a straight, controlled flight. For this reason, the comparatively inexperienced player needs to understand fully the way in which spin is imparted to the ball if she is to get rid of this unwanted sidespin.

A golf ball will fly straight, without curving away to right or left, only if the clubface is aimed in the same direction as it is travelling (fig. 1). To produce this 'square' clubface at impact is one of the prime aims of the good golfswing. In order to hit the golf ball on-target, not only must the swing be travelling on-target, but the clubface must also be looking at the target. Whenever the clubface and swing are at odds with one another – in other words, with the swing travelling in one direction but with the clubface aimed in another – a spin is immediately imparted to the ball. If clubface and swing converge, so that the clubface is aimed left and the swing to the right, a hookspin is produced so that the ball starts out to the right of target and hooks away to the left (fig. 2). Conversely, if the swingpath and clubface diverge, so that the swing travels left of target while the clubface is aimed to the right, the result is a slice – the ball starting left and curving away to the right (fig. 3).

9

Fig. 2   The 'closed' clubface which produces a hook

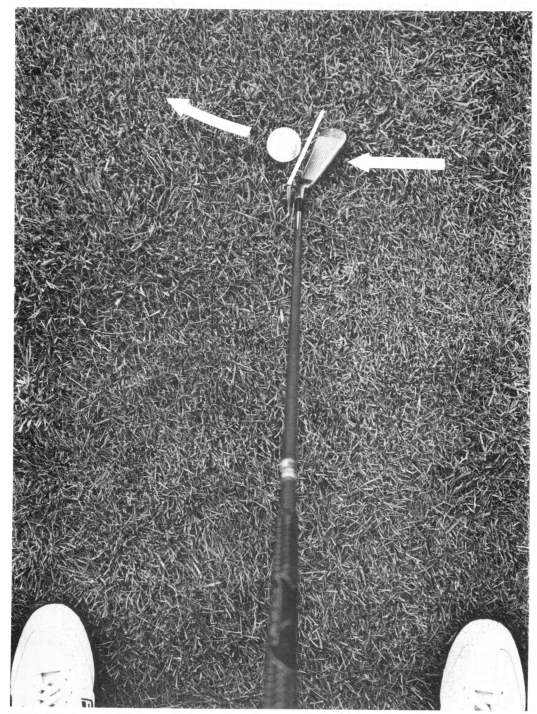

Fig. 3 The 'open' clubface which produces a slice

Most golfers do not find it easy to return the clubface to the ball in the square, on-target position. Most are prone to producing either a hookspin or a slicespin on the ball. These are not difficult faults to correct, *if* the player appreciates the reason for the shots. But most golfers simply do not understand with sufficient clarity why the ball spins one way or the other and therefore they try to correct the problem in a totally haphazard or misguided way. The golfer who continually sees her shots flying out to the right of target often does not appreciate that the ball is *curving* out there. She imagines that the ball is flying in a straight line away to the right. Her instinct tells her that, if the ball is travelling away to the right, she should aim her swing more to the left. If the ball *were* flying in a straight line, this would be logically correct. But, in fact, in trying to aim her swing more to the left, she sets the direction of her swing at even greater odds to the clubface position. Her slice on the ball increases and the ball travels even farther away to the right. This occurs simply through a lack of understanding of what produces the various kinds of shots in golf.

So, the first principle to grasp in learning to improve your golf is that it is largely a game of spin and curves. The golf ball does not easily fly in a straight line. As you improve in other sports you usually learn to put spin *on* a ball. In golf, the inexperienced player must learn to take the sidespin *off* the ball. For this reason, your instinctive reaction to the problem is very often entirely wrong. Corrections in golf are frequently entirely opposite to what you expect. Swinging to the left may make you hit the ball to the right; swinging to the right may make the ball curve left. It will probably seem entirely illogical until you understand the fundamentals and begin to appreciate the manner in which the ball flies.

The size of the ball

The second point which the golfer, particularly the near-novice, needs to understand is that golf is a difficult game because of the size of the ball. The ball is small; that is obvious. This raises a serious problem. With the golf ball sitting on the ground in front of you, the target area which you are trying to strike with the clubhead is a spot on the ground, less than half an inch in diameter, directly underneath the ball. That is your target. You have to swing the club up and behind your head, and then return it with sufficient accuracy to be able to brush the ground at this exact spot in order to strike the ball cleanly. Without plenty of practice, or an exceptionally good eye for the ball, this is an extremely demanding task.

When you look at inexperienced golfers you are likely to see that they learn to produce a reasonably good-looking swing without the ball; this practice swing *looks* as though it could be fairly effective. But, when they come to try the same swing with the ball, the initial result is appalling. The clubhead may strike the ball on its top; catch the ground several inches behind it; strike the ball from the toe or the heel of the club, or even miss the ball altogether.

Players immediately assume the swing is all wrong and try to change it – quite needlessly, merely because they have not appreciated the exceptional accuracy required from the swing. To make any sort of acceptable shot, the clubhead must strike the ground on the exact spot – the half inch target beneath the ball. An inch out at impact spells disaster.

The beginner needs to develop a fluent, reasonably orthodox-looking swing. But that is not all there is to striking the golf ball well. She then has to learn to make *that* swing strike the ground accurately in the right place. So often, players learn a fairly good-looking swing quite rapidly, but simply do not have any success at first because they do not understand the importance of the accuracy at impact. This is really the hard part of learning to play golf initially – learning to brush the ground beneath the ball; the basic swing itself is relatively simple.

Two key points

So there, then, are two key points. You are dealing with a game of spin and curves which needs to be understood if you are to hope for improvement. Secondly, you are dealing with a very small ball which requires an accuracy of contact which the inexperienced player can rarely achieve. This accuracy of contact must be worked at and is not something which automatically follows on from producing a good-looking swing.

Golf is not a simple game for the adult to learn, but with these two principles in mind so that you understand it a little better, it should fall into place rather more easily.

2 The grip

The golf grip serves two vital roles in the swing. Firstly, a good grip helps to produce power and distance to the shot. Secondly, and more important from the teaching point of view, it is fundamental in helping to produce the square clubface at impact, which I dealt with in Chapter 1. In other words, a good grip is important in bringing the club back to the ball, facing in the right direction. It is this which largely controls the direction of the shots and determines whether you hit the ball straight, or become prone to either of the common golfing faults – hooking and slicing.

Forming the grip

Keeping this principle in mind – that you are trying to return the clubface squarely to the ball – the first point is to start to form the grip with the clubface square to the target. In other words, the line along the front of the clubface should be facing on-target. That in itself sounds very easy, but players frequently fall into the habit of letting the club sit slightly open or shut – with the club set off to right or left. First, then, check the squareness of the clubface. Now hang the fingers of the left hand loosely down by the side of the top of the club, and then fold the hand over to take hold of it, leaving perhaps a quarter of an inch at the top of the grip. There are two key points here. Firstly, the tip of the thumb and first joint of the index finger should be roughly level with one another (fig. 4). What you should *not* see is the left thumb stretched too far down the club. This is quite wrong and will lead to trouble in putting the right hand on; it will be liable to loosen during the swing and may even cause a strain in the thumb itself. The hand should be in a position where the fingers are pointing very much down and along the club, with the thumb pulled up fairly short, though still well in contact with the club.

The second important point is the line between the thumb and index finger. The thumb and index finger should be kept very close together, down to the joint in the thumb, so as to form a nice, neat line. They should *not* be allowed to spread apart. As you look down at your grip, this line between the thumb and index finger should seem to point back up towards the right ear or right shoulder. This means that the left hand is slightly on top of the club and will probably allow you to see the first two knuckles of the left hand, and possibly part of the third. The positioning of this line is important.

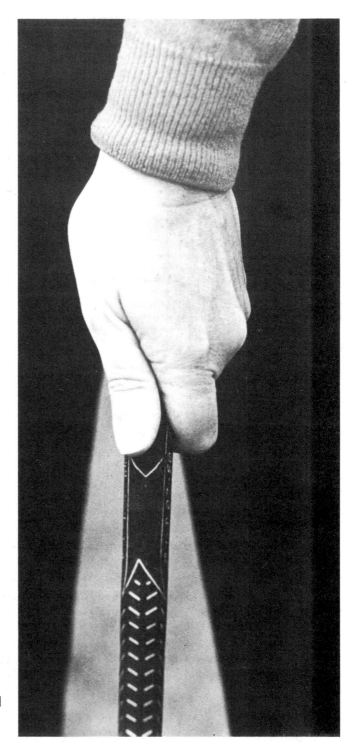

Fig. 4 Line between left thumb and index finger pointing to the right shoulder

Adding the right hand

With the left hand in position, let's look at the way the right hand is added. The most widely taught grip is known as the 'Vardon grip' or overlapping grip. In this, the little finger of the right hand fits over the index finger of the left, keeping the two hands working very much in unison. To form this grip, separate the little finger of the right hand from the other three. If you find this separation easy, the grip will probably seem straightforward; if not, it will feel cumbersome. Having pulled the little finger away from the other three, rest the club in the middle joints of the three fingers of the right hand. Then draw the right hand up so that the fold in the base of the palm of the right hand fits snugly against the left thumb. This will mean that the right hand is now diagonally on the club, the fingers pointing – if they were extended – down the shaft (fig. 5). Now fold the right hand over to cover up the left thumb, which should fit easily into the fleshy part of the right palm, and be entirely hidden from view (fig. 6). The little finger of the right hand should then fit over or round the joint of the index finger of the left – whichever feels the more comfortable (fig. 7).

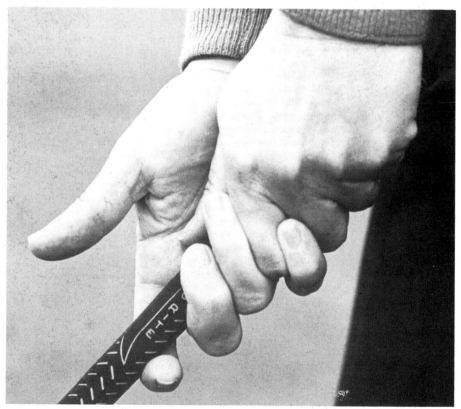

Fig. 5   Adding the right hand – club resting in the fingers

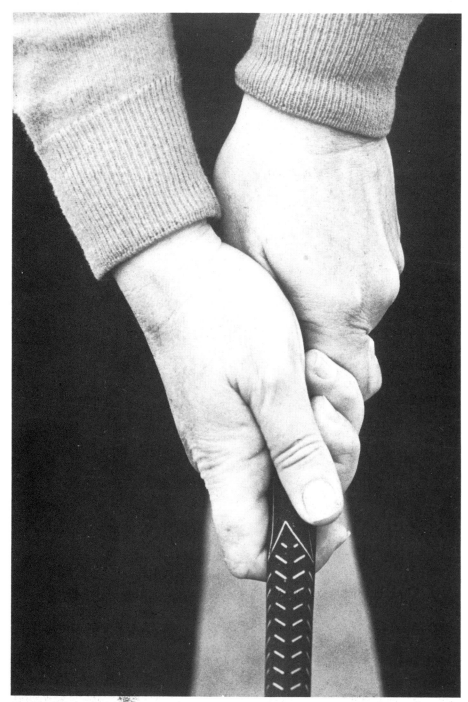

Fig. 6   The lines between thumb and index finger pointing to the right shoulder

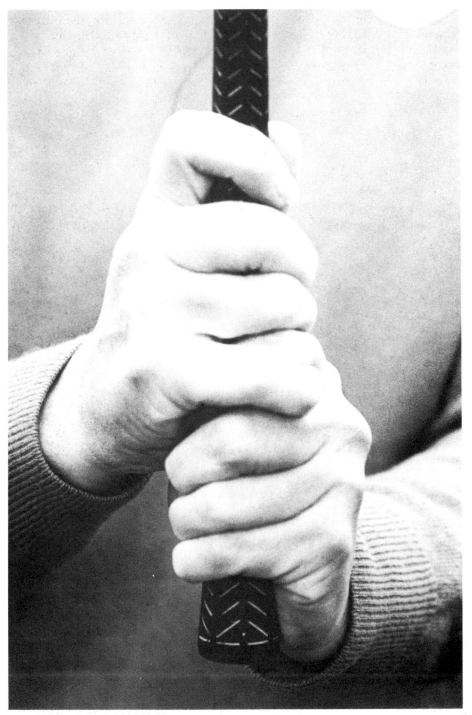

Fig. 7a The overlapping grip. Notice the right forefinger position

In adjusting the right hand to produce exactly the correct grip, there are two key points very similar to those which applied to the left hand. Once more, the tip of the thumb should be virtually level with the first joint of the index finger – not with the thumb stretched down along the club. Both thumbs, although in contact with the club, should be well pulled up. The second key to a good right-hand grip is a similar line between thumb and index finger to the one seen in the left hand. In the right hand, the thumb and index finger will separate away from each other rather more than with the left hand, but there should still be a very distinct line. Once again, it should seem to you, in looking at your own grip, that the line points up somewhere between your right ear and right shoulder (fig. 6).

Fig. 7b Side view of the overlapping grip

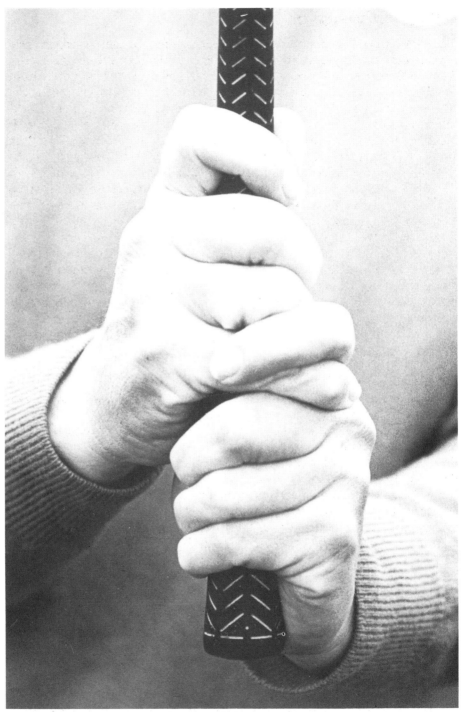

Fig. 8   The interlocking grip, fingertips linked

Alternative grips

The Vardon grip is not suitable for every golfer. It can be particularly troublesome to the person whose little finger does not easily separate away from the others. In this case, it is often hard to pull the little finger away from the others sufficiently to feel comfortable in overlapping it around the index finger of the left hand. In this case, a better alternative is often the 'interlocking grip' – which is the one used by Jack Nicklaus. Many professionals, myself included, will often teach this to beginners because it is, perhaps, a little more simple to learn at first. In this grip, the index finger of the left hand and the little finger of the right hand are hooked together, both fingertips outwards (fig. 8). A word of warning here. The two linked fingers should not be linked right to the bottom of each finger; only the tips of the fingers hook together.

The other alternative is the two-handed baseball grip, where all eight fingers are on the club, without any overlapping or interlocking. It is not really a grip I would recommend to beginners. The weakness is that the hands tend to slide apart and work against one another instead of together and in harmony. However, it *can* be the best grip for the player with really small hands or for the older player who gradually finds difficulty with either of the others.

Adjusting the grip

I said at the beginning of this chapter that one of the main functions of a good grip is that of returning the clubface squarely to the ball. This must be a prime aim of every golfswing when a straight shot is required.

The reason I stressed the two lines between the thumb and index finger of either hand is that it is the positioning of the hands and adjustments of these lines which largely determine whether or not the clubface is returned squarely. With the hands in the orthodox position – both lines pointing up somewhere towards the right ear or shoulder – the two hands are very much to the sides of the club. Most people's hands, in swinging a golf club, will come through impact in this type of position, with the hands predominantly to the sides – left palm facing right, right palm facing left. If you start with the hands in this position on the club, they will usually return in the same position, returning the clubface to the ball in the square position in which it started at address.

If, on the other hand, the right hand is very much underneath the club, with the line in the right hand pointing outside the right shoulder, if visible at all, it will tend to return in a different position from the one in which it started (figs. 9 and 10). As the right hand approaches impact it turns to face the target, 'closing' the clubface, so that it looks left of target, thus producing a shot which hooks away to the left. The added problem here is that, as the clubface is turned into a left-aimed position, the loft of the club is effectively reduced and the ball flies off with a lower trajectory than normal. Much the same

Fig. 9 Incorrect grip at address

Fig. 10 A strong grip tends to close the clubface at impact

pattern of shot will follow if the left hand is too much on top of the club. Again, it will return to impact in a different position, bringing the clubface in closed.

The problem for many players is that this 'strong' or 'hooker's' grip often feels much more powerful than the correct grip. The club is very largely supported by the right hand and this tends to give the impression of strength and power. What you should feel in a good grip – particularly if you have this type of fault – is that the right hand is kept very much *behind* the club and not underneath it. After all, you want the power in the hand aimed on-target. Having the right hand very much underneath tends to make the novice golfer feel that she is able in some way to lift the ball into the air rather more easily than with the orthodox grip. In fact, it does just the reverse. The right hand in this position will bring the clubface in with its effective loft reduced, so that it is even harder to get the ball airborne. For the player who finds real difficulty in getting sufficient height with the fairway woods, long irons and the driver, it is often worth looking at the grip – quite frequently you will find that the right hand is unsuitably underneath, so that the loft of the clubface is being reduced through impact.

While, in theory, having the right hand predominantly under the club, with the lines between thumb and index finger pointing right of the shoulder, does produce a hook, what must be pointed out is that in extreme cases it can cause other problems. If the right hand is in an ultra-strong position, with the right thumb very much behind the shaft of the club, it is possible for the player to immobilise her wrists to such an extent through impact that all the power is generated with the right thumb and the clubface is left wide open, leading to a bad slice. While theoretically this type of grip always produces a hook, in practice the extreme case can produce a slice.

Conversely, if the lines between thumb and index finger of either hand or both hands point to the chin or left of it, the clubface will be returned to the ball in an 'open' position and the ball will slice away to the right of target (figs. 11 and 12). This type of 'weak' grip is relatively common in the left hand amongst beginners, who find it unnatural to set the left hand slightly on top of the club, but it is also fairly common in reasonably low-handicap players who have perhaps over-corrected from a hooker's grip in the past. A word of warning here for the low-handicap player. If the left-hand grip is allowed to weaken too much in an attempt to counteract a tendency to hook, so that the guideline points left of the chin, there is a danger of the left hand becoming so weak through impact that it cannot stand up to the power of the right, and simply collapses under the strain. This can produce a worse hook. So, a weak grip – with the lines of either or both hands pointing left of the chin – in theory produces a slice. In practice, however, it is possible for an extremely weak position to produce a hook.

Fig. 11 Incorrect grip at address

Fig. 12 A weak grip produces an open clubface at impact

Tension in the grip

One of the points about the grip which seems to cause a great deal of argument is just how tightly you should hold a golf club. The problem is that the strength of people's hands varies to such an extent that a grip that is tight to you may be a relatively loose grip for another player and vice versa. What you do want from a grip is that it should be sufficiently relaxed to enable the wrists to stay loose and free to produce power in the swing. Gripping too tightly usually tends to slice the ball, because of much too much tension in the wrists – immobilising them through impact.

On the other hand, very many players produce a grip which actually loosens throughout the swing, often becoming loose through impact and allowing the club to twist as it strikes the ball. This is particularly noticeable with the long irons and in recovery shots. You want a grip which gives maximum freedom in the wrists throughout the swing, yet which has the club firmly under control as it strikes the ball.

Probably the best exercise to strengthen the hands and to ensure that the grip stays constant is to line up a row of four or five balls and to hit them one after the other without re-gripping the club. Hit the first ball, then step forward and address the next; hit that without moving the hands, then address the next and hit that and so on. If you can train yourself to move through four or five balls without getting any movement in the hands, you can be sure the grip is beginning to work correctly.

Another problem which is associated with the tension of the grip is the size of the grip you should use on clubs. From my own experience, any tendency towards having too thin a grip on the club will usually result in the club being held too tightly. A thick grip on the club, on the other hand, makes it difficult for the player to hold the club correctly and should be avoided most definitely by the player who is learning. A reasonably thin grip is probably easier to hold correctly – provided it is not so thin as to produce excessive tension.

The key points

To sum up then, both hands should be positioned with the fingers pointing very much *along* the club, with the thumbs pulled up reasonably short. The lines between the thumb and index finger of both hands should seem to point up somewhere between your right ear and shoulder. The more these lines are turned to the right, the more likely you are to hook the ball, or less likely to slice it. Conversely, the farther these lines point to the left, the more prone you will be to slicing the ball, and so less likely to hook it.

3 Setting up for success

One of the problems about golf is that the basics of the game – the grip and stance – need to be kept under constant surveillance. No golfer ever gets to the stage where she can safely say that faults will not creep into these most elementary parts of her game. In most other ball games the basics become ingrained and are forgotten. In golf, you must never ignore the fundamentals.

The stance, in particular, is a common source of error. Few golfers set up consistently day after day. Their direction and alignment alter, the distance from the ball changes and very often the whole posture varies sufficiently to cause problems. The stance needs constant supervision. But, in order to keep it in check, you need to understand the exact functions of the stance and to be familiar with the types of changes which are likely to lead to error.

The stance – front view

One of the two main purposes of the set-up is to enable the player to swing the club to the top of the backswing as simply as possible. (The other main function of the set-up is direction; more about that later.) The better the set-up the more likely the golfer is to be able to produce a good, repetitive backswing.

Let us start with a really basic set-up with a 6- or 7-iron. First of all, you should position yourself with the ball opposite the centre of your feet, with the feet together. Now put your feet apart, left foot first and then the right, so that the ball is still roughly opposite the centre. The feet should be sufficiently wide apart for the weight to feel slightly on the insides of the feet, toes turned out a little – the left probably rather more than the right. It is important to get this feeling of having the weight towards the inside of the feet. For most women, the best guide is usually to feel that the feet are hip width. A stance for a woman which is too narrow in relation to her hips will usually lead to poor legwork and loss of balance in the backswing. The knees, in turn, should be knocked in a little, and relaxed though *not* forcibly bent (fig. 13).

The positioning of the arms at address is vital in producing the best possible backswing. In swinging the club back, the left arm has to stay straight, while the right arm folds into the body. To achieve this most easily, the left arm should be hanging perfectly straight at address – but hanging loosely and *not* tense. The right hand is below the left in the grip. This means that the right shoulder should be allowed to drop quite naturally several inches below the

28

Fig. 13   The medium iron address

left shoulder at address. The right arm should then be relaxed, the elbow dropped into the body; this will enable it to fold away quite simply on the backswing.

It is worth paying some extra attention to the position of the arms – especially the left one. In watching almost all top-class golfers, you will notice that the inside of the left arm is clearly visible, so that the left elbow is pointing diagonally downwards and *not* straight out towards the target. This is important. If too much tension is created in the left arm so that the elbow points directly towards the target, the arm will be unable to fold away neatly in the throughswing as it should and will produce a blocking action, with a tendency to push the ball out to the right. So, although the left arm must be kept reasonably straight at address, you should make sure that it is in a loose position, with the elbow slightly downwards. The right arm, too, should follow this same pattern – with the inside of the arm visible.

The ball position

In looking at the set-up from the front, the other point to clarify is the exact position of the ball in relation to the feet. I have started by using the most basic address position, where the ball is kept centrally in the feet when using a medium iron. But there is rather more to the ball position than this. In fact, keeping the ball correctly positioned is one of the major problems for many really top-class players. It is something which alters all too easily, and yet, of course, is not that easy to check for yourself. As you look down at the ball in relation to your feet, your own view is slightly distorted and you will probably not get a sufficiently true picture to make the necessary adjustments. This is therefore something which often needs assistance from a professional or a playing partner.

There are two basic things which determine where you should position your feet in relation to the ball. The first is the way in which you swing and the second is the type of lie on which the ball sits and hence the contact you want to produce.

Let us look first at the way in which your swing will determine the ball position you need. The simple principle is this. You need to position the ball at the point which corresponds to the bottom of your swing. For the average club golfer, certainly for the older player and for the vast majority of women players, the bottom of the swing will most naturally fall at a point opposite the player's nose – roughly in the middle of the stance. It makes sense, therefore, to think in terms of positioning the ball somewhere in this area – making it as easy as possible to contact the ball.

In the case of the top-class golfer and the younger player, the bottom of the swing is more likely to fall at a spot which is nearer the left foot. This is brought about by faster hand action, and more speed in the legs. It therefore makes sense for the better golfer to have the ball nearer the left foot than the average club golfer will. The simple way to check this is to have a number of practice swings and see just where the bottom of the swing is falling. If it naturally falls somewhere opposite the middle of the stance, this should be the basic position around which variations should be made. If the natural bottom of the swing is farther towards the left foot, then this will determine your ideal type of ball position. But bear in mind that this is the reason why the ball position advocated by the top-class tournament professional is not *usually* the one for the average club golfer.

The next point to consider is the type of contact with the ball that is required, for this, in turn, will mean making some adjustment to the ball position. There are three basic contacts required in golf. In some cases you need to catch the ball before the club reaches the bottom of the swing – a downward contact. In some instances, you want to catch the ball right at the bottom of the swing, and in others you need to catch the ball when the club has passed the bottom of the swing and is therefore travelling slightly upwards.

For short iron shots, or from a tight or bare lie, or in most kinds of recovery shot, you need to hit the ball with the club still travelling downwards. In other words, you want to catch the ball with a descending blow, taking the ball and then a small divot beyond it. For this type of contact, the ball must be played slightly farther towards the right foot than in your basic ball position. This will encourage you to strike the ball on the downswing – ball first and then the turf.

For the ordinary type of lie, where the ball sits on a little grass, the ball should be struck right from the bottom of the swing; from your basic ball position.

On the other hand, when the ball is teed up for a drive, the idea is to catch the ball slightly on the upswing – after the club has reached its lowest point. To encourage this, the ball must be played farther to the left than your basic ball position – for the club golfer a couple of inches inside the left heel and for the better player even as far to the left as to be opposite the left toes. The clubhead will now reach its lowest point somewhere opposite the middle of the stance and strike the ball on the upswing.

The main points about the ball position are therefore these. Firstly, from a number of practice swings find out where the natural bottom of your own swing is. Having found this, adjust yourself to the ball position accordingly. When you want a downward contact with a short iron or from a bad lie, position the ball behind this spot, that is, farther to the right. If the ball is sitting very well and when it is teed up with a driver, an upward contact is required – so, position the ball farther towards the left foot to encourage this. The hands should stay roughly in the same position in relation to your body, so that they will be noticeably ahead of the ball when the downward contact is required, and may be slightly behind the ball when the upward contact is being produced with a driver.

The stance – side view

In looking at the stance from the side, we are really concerned with two factors – posture and direction. As you stand to the golf ball, the feeling should be one of standing up tall. All bending should come from the top of the legs, *not* from the waist or by drooping in the back. The feeling must be one of keeping the hips up and sticking the bottom out slightly. Once this has been done, the knees can be flexed a little (fig. 14). The arms then hang in a relaxed manner, so that there is a slight angle between the arms and shaft of the club.

Fig. 14 Correct posture: standing tall, bottom out

Many club golfers adopt an entirely unsuitable posture in setting-up to the ball. The common tendency is to droop at the knees – which means that the player loses height and adopts too much of a sitting position (fig. 15). This is quite wrong. What has happened here is that the hips have been allowed to drop as the knees have bent. The player has sat down, rather than having kept the hips up. This leads to two major faults. Either the player will rise up through impact, straightening her left leg and raising her whole body, or she will simply find that because her hips are dropped there is insufficient space for her legs to work properly, so that the left leg crumples out of the way

Fig. 15 Incorrect posture: legs too bent, shoulders drooped

Fig. 16 Incorrect posture: with legs too bent at address, this is the
natural result

through impact (fig. 16). At address the hips must be kept up and back in order to give the legs space to work. For the very tall player, it is essential to keep this feeling of sticking the bottom out – then allowing the knees to bend – rather than simply drooping and losing height unnecessarily.

Distance from the ball

The type of posture you adopt determines to a large extent the distance you stand from the ball. The more you bend over, the farther you are likely to stand from the ball; the more upright your posture, the closer you will stand. As a general rule, most top-class golfers are able to stand very much closer to the ball than the average club golfer. The closer you are able to stand, the easier it is to swing the club on a straight path through impact and thus the better the direction you are likely to produce. By contrast, the player who stands a long way from the ball produces a sharply curved path through impact, resulting in erratic direction (fig. 17). Most higher-handicap golfers feel much more comfortable standing farther from the ball than they should. As you strive for improvement, it is generally necessary to stand in closer, sticking the bottom out, so that the lower part of the body is kept out of the way to give the arms space to swing.

To check your distance from the ball, I would suggest that you ask someone else to stand in your footprints in order to get a true picture of your set-up and the type of distance you adopt. Also, watch most really good professionals and you will probably be aware of just how close they play the ball to their feet – almost certainly much closer than the club golfer.

Direction

The set-up is vital in producing the right direction to shots. A poor position not only leads to badly aimed shots, but also, as a rule, to some sort of counteraction in the swing so that all sorts of other faults result. The basic set-up is the 'square' position. All this really means is that, if you take a straight line from the ball to the target, the line across the toes, knees, hips and shoulders should all be parallel to this line – like a pair of railway lines. This is not always easy to achieve – the best way of checking your own stance is simply to lay another club down along your toes to get some idea of the direction. Most golfers who do not easily aim correctly adopt a position where the line across the feet runs away to the right of target, often as much as 30 degrees off line. From here, the golfer will usually either push shots away to the right or will compensate for her set-up in some way and turn on the shot and pull the ball to the left. The more she turns and pulls the ball to the left, the more she aims away to the right – gradually producing all sorts of faults in the swing.

For the player who does not line up correctly – and very few do – the solution is to adopt a set routine in order to produce the right address position and direction to the stance. I suggest the following. Stand directly behind the

Fig. 17 Standing too far away produces erratic direction

ball, facing your target. Now choose a spot on the ground, perhaps 18 inches (46 cm) in front of the ball, directly on-line with the target. Keeping this spot in mind, walk round to address the ball and simply concentrate on aiming the clubface out over this spot, giving yourself an imaginary line from the ball to the spot. Then concentrate on setting the feet, hips and shoulders parallel to this line as you take up your stance. Having adopted this position, you may find it easiest *not* to look up at the target again, in case you *feel* to be set-up incorrectly, but simply to concentrate on hitting the ball out over your spot on the ground. In this way, you will soon learn to adopt a square stance – repeating this pattern for everything from short irons to drives.

However, there is another important point about the set-up. Although I have stressed the line across the feet, it is almost more important to keep the line across the shoulders aimed correctly. It is the way in which the shoulders turn throughout the swing which really controls the direction of shots, and to encourage the right direction, the shoulders should, for most golfers, start on the same parallel line as the feet. Unfortunately, this is not as simple as it sounds. Because the right hand is below the left on the grip, it also means that the right hand is slightly forward of the left. This means that there is a tendency for the right arm to pull the right shoulder forward, instead of allowing it to drop down below the left as it should. The majority of golfers need to feel, quite consciously, that the right shoulder is kept pulled back in order to keep the shoulders on-line. If the right shoulder moves forward in the set-up, so that the shoulder line is aimed left, this tends to set the line of the swing across the desired direction of the shot. This *usually* leads to a cutting-across action, putting a slice spin on the ball. To avoid this, the right shoulder must be kept back and down, not up and forward.

4 The basic golfswing

A dangerous tendency in learning to play golf is to break the golfswing down into too many pieces. It is all too easy to look at a sequence of pictures of the swing and to assume that the swing is made up of a number of stages and positions. I must stress to every golfer that the swing is a *swing*. It should be thought of as being a fluent movement, involving all parts of the body working in harmony and *not* a sequence of disjointed movements, working from one set position to another. If you think of the golfswing as a series of pictures you will ultimately produce a disjointed swing, which will always lack the apparent simplicity and fluency of the good player.

So, you must first have a very good picture of the *whole* swing. From this, you can go on to extract pieces upon which to work, but these pieces must be put back into the whole swing before some other piece is extracted for attention. Never try to learn a swing piece by piece.

The second point which you must grasp, in order to develop your golf correctly, is the true aim of the golfswing. What, after all, are you trying to do? The ultimate objective, of course, is to hit the ball to the target down the fairway. I say 'of course', for one would think every golfer would have this as her primary aim in swinging the club. But too often golfers lose sight of this primary objective and work far too much on the appearance or technique of the swing, without bearing in mind that the whole purpose behind it is that of getting the ball from A to B in the most reliable and repetitive manner possible.

In the actual golfswing itself, you are trying to swing the club up and behind the head, and, from there, generating speed and swinging the club through, so that the clubhead strikes the ball as it brushes the ground, and travels on through to complete its full circular path as the speed decreases. You are aiming at swinging the *clubhead* in a circle, so that it travels in the right direction, brushes the ground at the spot where the ball is and imparts maximum speed to the ball in so doing.

This sounds basic and simple. But you must appreciate and remember that the aim of the swing is to swing the clubhead. It is the clubhead which should be kept very much in mind. Concentrate on moving the clubhead in the right path and the body and arms will very largely follow and produce the right movements in doing so. Far too many golfers forget what should be happening to the club and concentrate entirely on the way in which the body and arms move instead. This is wrong. Aim at letting the body and arms move in sympathy with the clubhead as it travels its correct path, rather than thinking of the body and arms and imagining the club will follow correctly. Swing the clubhead, and let the body move with it.

The simple swing

The way I like to describe the golfswing is in terms of two very simple movements. It is really just a combination of two things. Firstly, the body simply moves and turns to the right and then turns through to the left, letting the feet move quite freely as it turns. Secondly, the arms swing up to the right, down and up to the left. Thus, it is a turn of the body and a swing of the arms. To develop a basic golfswing, all you have to do is to put the two together. Turn to the right and lift the arms up. Turn to the left and swing the arms down and up. Without a golf club in the hands, this is easy; but there, basically, is the simple swing. Exactly the same should follow with a club in the hands. You turn the body to the right and lift the arms and club, supporting the club on the left thumb at the top of the swing. From there, turn the body through to the left, swinging the club down and lifting the arms to the other side: again, turn to the right and swing the arms up; turn to the left and swing the arms up (figs. 18 and 19).

The way in which your golfswing develops is largely a matter of timing these two movements together, and maintaining – however sophisticated your idea of the swing becomes – the basic concept of a turn of the body, combined with a lift of the arms. The golfer who never develops a good-looking swing usually either turns the body without producing the necessary lift in the arms, or lifts the arms without producing the turning movement in the body. Her swing becomes one movement instead of two.

I suggest that you maintain this simple picture as a kind of framework into which every piece of golfing knowledge is slotted. It is so easy to learn intricacies of the swing as your game develops, without keeping the idea of the whole swing in which they are supposed to fit. So this simple idea – the turn and lift concept – is the one to return to whenever your game reaches a crisis point and there is a danger of becoming overwhelmed by theory.

Let us remind ourselves again of the simple ideas with which we are setting out to develop the golfswing. Firstly, the whole object of the swing is to move the clubhead, at maximum speed, in a circular path, the bottom of which coincides with the position of the ball, and the direction of which is going where you are trying to hit the ball. Secondly, it is the clubhead which should be your main concern so that you swing that and let the arms and body move in sympathy with it. Thirdly, remember that when you do have to think of the body and arms they move in two separate ways. The body turns from side to side while the arms swing up and down and up to the other side. When in doubt and difficulty return to these three basic principles to give you the correct framework within which to work.

Fig.18   Turn the body and then lift the arms in the backswing

Fig. 19 Swish the club down, then turn on through and lift the arms again. Turn and lift; turn and lift

5 Developing the backswing

In looking at the development of a really good swing, it is logical to start by talking about the backswing. This is not, in my view, because it is the most important part of the golfswing. On the contrary, I think there is a danger in overstressing the importance of the backswing. The part of the golfswing which hits the ball is, after all, the throughswing, so my own feeling is that it is the throughswing to which most attention should be paid. There are, to be fair, two different schools of thought on this. The first school will say, 'If you can swing the club correctly to the top of the backswing, all the important work has been done and a good throughswing will follow.' I do not agree with this. Many players swing the club back well enough to the top of the swing, and never then make an adequate pass at the ball.

The other school of thought, and the one to which I strongly adhere, is that the backswing simply sets you up ready to execute the throughswing, which is the primary part of the swing and the one on which most importance should be placed. This is very much my philosophy in teaching. The backswing is, of course, important – but to a limited degree. For the club golfer, the backswing is important to the extent that it is preparatory for executing the down and throughswing. But months and months of work developing the club golfer's backswing will probably not do anything to improve her swing through the ball.

The stages I believe you should work through are these. Firstly, develop an *acceptable* backswing – one which points the club in the right direction and creates sufficient potential energy to strike the ball – without being too fussy. You can then remain uninhibited. From there, learn to perfect the throughswing as far as possible, striving at improving the overall direction and striking of the ball. Very often – and I would stress the importance of realising this – working at improvement in the throughswing leads backwards to raising the standard of the backswing. Having learnt to swing the club in a repetitive, reliable manner through the ball, you are then ready to polish up the whole technique by making the fine adjustments which can go on in the backswing. But at this stage, we are talking of transforming the 12-handicap golfer into a 4-handicap, or the club assistant into a champion. The real intricacies of the backswing should not be meddled with by the relatively long-handicap player. For her, the aim should be an acceptable backswing, followed by perfection through the ball – *not* perfection in the backswing, followed by a non-existent, inhibited throughswing, as is the usual case.

A simple backswing

Bearing in mind, therefore, that the backswing is only preparatory to the throughswing, let us look at how it should be developed. What you are aiming at doing in the backswing is to swing the club up and behind the head, so that it points parallel to the desired flight of the shot. The body turns and the arms lift, making it as easy as possible to swing the club at speed through the ball in the right direction.

The overall picture of the backswing should be this. The shoulders should turn *on a fairly horizontal plane*, while the arms – and predominantly the left arm – lift the club. This, then, is what we are aiming at in the top of the backswing position. The shoulders have turned, the left arm is very much in control and supporting the club and the shaft of the club points down the proposed line of flight of the ball (figs. 20 to 24).

Rather than work stage by stage through the swing, which tends to lead the club player to fragment the swing to too great a degree, it is easier to isolate the various parts of the body and the feelings you need in them to build a repetitive and sound backswing.

Fig. 20 The address position – everything ready for the backswing and, in turn, the shot

Fig. 21

Fig. 22

Fig. 23

Fig. 24

Figs. 20–24 The backswing should be largely left side dominant. The left side of the body turns to the right – the shoulders being rounded at the top of the backswing – with the left arm in control and the club being supported on the left thumb

Let us look at the left arm and hand. Most good golfers – if not all – will agree that the left arm and, indeed, the left side, should be very much in control throughout the backswing. The left arm, after all, has to be straight and extended in the backswing in order to create the necessary width to the arc. My own feeling is very much of swinging the left arm tightly across my chest *to the right shoulder*. The space between the left arm and right shoulder at the top of the backswing for the good golfer is usually comparatively small, despite there being no bend in the left arm. In order to develop this movement and control in the left arm you need to work, as a rule, on two exercises.

Firstly, any aspiring golfer should be able to swing a medium iron with perfect control, from address to the top of the backswing, with the left arm alone. In order to develop this control, it is perhaps easier to start with the left thumb rather more on top of the club than in the ordinary grip, so that you definitely feel the left thumb in a supporting position as the club reaches the top of the swing. The best exercise is to swing the club, comparatively slowly, from address to the top of the backswing and then down to address again, quite slowly. Do not bother with the throughswing. Just swing the club back

Fig. 25 The exercise for producing left arm freedom

and then down to address; back and down to address – perhaps 30 times to make a suitable exercise.

The second exercise is aimed at freeing up the muscles and tendons in the back of the left shoulder so that you can swing the left arm freely up to the right shoulder. Hold the left arm out in front of you, palm of the hand downwards. Now, with the right hand behind the left elbow, pull the left arm across towards the right shoulder, keeping the arm perfectly straight (fig. 25). The majority of adults beginning to use this exercise will find it virtually impossible to keep the left arm straight and to draw it across to touch the right shoulder. If you have not got this kind of freedom, it is impossible to produce a backswing in which the left arm is drawn tightly across towards the right shoulder as the professional does. Either the left arm will bend slightly, losing width and leading to a variable backswing, or the space between the left arm and right shoulder is likely to be unsuitably large.

So, as far as the left arm is concerned, it is very much a question of drawing the left arm across to the right shoulder in the backswing and of having the left arm in control, with the right arm relatively passive.

The shoulder turn

There are two aspects to the shoulder turn which I would isolate – firstly, the way in which the two shoulders work together and, secondly, the plane on which the shoulders move.

Just as the arms should be working with the left one in a dominant position and the right in a passive state, so the shoulder action should be dominated by the left shoulder, rather than the right. You might fall into the trap, and justifiably so, of thinking that turning the shoulders would result in the same movement whether you thought in terms of turning with the right shoulder or turning with the left. But this is not so. If you concentrate on turning with the left shoulder, it produces an entirely different result from turning with the right shoulder. If you initiate the shoulder turn with the left shoulder, this means that the left shoulder is rounding itself into the right, so that the back is rounded. In other words the left shoulder moves *to* the right shoulder. This is what should happen, so that at the top of the backswing, the shoulders are rounded. If, on the other hand, you think of turning away with the right shoulder, the chest is extended and the shoulder blades pushed back. This is quite wrong. You must feel that the left shoulder initiates the turn on the backswing, drawing it into the right shoulder so that the back is rounded. There, again, it is very much a question of left side control.

The second important aspect of the shoulder turn is the plane on which the shoulders move. Again you need to come back to the simple basic principle of turning the body and lifting the arms. We are looking at two movements. The shoulders should therefore turn on a relatively horizontal plane while the lifting action is provided by the arms – in particular the left one. The golfer who finds problems with the backswing usually makes only one movement instead of the two. Either she forces the left shoulder *down* in order to get the club up, instead of lifting the arms, or swings the whole body plus the arms round in a horizontal baseball-type plane, without producing the necessary lift.

Correctly, the shoulders and left arm must be on a completely different plane at the top of the swing – with the left shoulder kept high and the shoulder plane very nearly horizontal, while the lift in the swing is provided by the left arm (fig. 26). Once you develop this kind of position, the arms are able to swing down and through the ball, without too much unwanted influence and power from the shoulders.

Fig. 26 The shoulder plane should always be flatter than the arm plane

The leg action

What I would always suggest to relative beginners at golf is that they give plenty of freedom to the legs. Let the legs work and move quite freely to develop fluency in the swing and then, if necessary, cut down on the leg action in order to build a more solid and reliable swing. But, first, be relatively uninhibited and give yourself freedom. In order to produce the necessary turn with the left shoulder, the newer golfer will usually have to let the hips turn in the backswing, allowing the left heel to pull a couple of inches off the ground in so doing. Do not be afraid to let this happen. It is not something one sees as a rule in the top-class professional, but the club golfer needs to give herself all the freedom possible to get the club up to the top of the backswing, with the back facing the target as it should.

As your golf develops, the left leg is likely to move rather less in the backswing. As the left shoulder turns, the left side of the body will come forward, so that the weight on the left foot should move from being flat on the foot to being on the ball of the foot. As it does so, the left knee will come forward and, being knocked in slightly at address, will seem to point roughly towards the ball. But the important thing here is the left foot. In the backswing, the weight is transferred *forward* in the foot. If that pulls the heel slightly off the ground, well and good. If not, it does not matter. What you should not strive to do is to keep the left heel firmly planted on the ground, *unless* you can still be sure that the weight transference onto the front of the foot is not being inhibited. Remember, the action of the left foot is *not* one of rolling onto the inside of the foot; it is a matter of weight moving forward in the foot, from the whole of the foot onto the ball of the foot.

The hand action

During the backswing, the hands have to move from a position where the wrists are only slightly cocked into one where they are fully cocked in order to produce maximum power. I say that they start in a slightly cocked position. In the address position, the hands are not held up at their highest point, with the club shaft and arms in a perfectly straight line. Instead, they are dropped very slightly. This angle is the beginning of the wristcock. All that really happens in the backswing is that the wrists hinge upwards so that the angle between the left thumb and the left arm approximates to a right angle. It is this movement which must take place as the arms swing to the top of the backswing. My own opinion is that it is undesirable to think too much of how, exactly, the wrists do cock in the backswing. Basically, all that should happen is that this angle is created gradually throughout the backswing, the movement being set in motion right from the takeaway, and the hinging action taking place quite gradually – not with a sudden jerk here or there.

If you think simply in terms of this hinging up movement, the club should be supported on the left thumb at the top of the backswing, with a slight angle

Fig. 27 The correct wrist position at the top of the backswing

in the back of the left hand, and the right hand folded completely back on itself (fig. 27). The right hand must, at this point, still be well in contact with the left thumb, covering it perfectly as at address.

For the player who has problems with the feeling of the wristcock, the best advice is not to think – or, at least, to try not to think – of anything between the address position and the top of the backswing. Simply think of taking your hands from A to B and do not worry about the route by which they get there.

Anyone who has a problem with the wristcock is usually suffering only from a mental problem of not being able to forget about it! I suggest, however, that if you have difficulties, you should alter the height of the hands at address. The lower the hands at address, the more of the wristcock you have already done. The higher the hands, the more there is left to do in the backswing. Experimenting very slightly on these lines is probably the best way of removing any discomfort and awkwardness with the hand action and wrist-cock.

The club position

Having learnt that the primary purpose of the golfswing is to move the clubhead in the right path, you should have a fairly good idea of the clubhead position you are aiming for at the top of the backswing. The direction in which the shaft of the club points at the top of the backswing determines to a certain extent the likely direction of the whole path of the throughswing. Ideally, the club should point in a line parallel to the proposed line of the shot (fig. 27). If the club points away to the left of this line – a 'laid-off' position – the downswing is likely to follow this left-aimed direction. Conversely, if the club points right of target, you are likely to attack the ball with a similarly right-aimed throughswing.

The direction which you produce at the top of the backswing is controlled by several factors – the degree to which you turn the shoulders, the suppleness of the arms and the direction of the start of the backswing. It is this last point – the direction of the takeaway – which is the key to producing a suitable direction at the top of the backswing. Many golfers fail to realise that the clubhead *must* be swung away from the ball in a curved path and *not* along a straight line extended back along the target-line. After all, your body is in the centre of a circular swing and the very first part of the backswing *must* set the club onto this circular path. The club must therefore move back *inside* the target-line. The more inside the club is taken in the takeaway, the more likely you are to produce a backswing where the club points on-target or slightly right of it. The straighter back the club is taken in the takeaway, the greater the likelihood there is of it aiming left of target at the top of the backswing.

In order to produce the right type of backswing you should, therefore, feel that the club is taken away on the inside and then, after this first movement, is lifted with the arms. In other words, we come back to our basic 'turn and lift' concept. It requires a combination of two movements – the turn of the body which brings the club back on the inside and the lift of the arms in order to achieve the required height to the backswing. The way in which you combine these two movements determines the type of backswing produced. A turn without a lift will lead to a flat plane in the swing, while lifting without the initial turn is likely to produce a very upright plane of swing.

You must keep very clearly in mind the picture of the swing as being the combination of these two movements – turn the body and lift the arms. To produce the desired direction at the top of the backswing and in the shots themselves, it is largely a case of experimenting slightly with the direction of the first few inches of the swing – pulling the club a little farther *inside* the target-line to correct a left-aimed path of swing, and pulling it slightly less inside to correct a right-aimed backswing.

6 Swinging through the ball

Having learnt to swing the club up to the top of the backswing in an acceptable position, you now come to the real crux of the swing – learning to swing the club on through and to contact the ball correctly. However good your backswing, it will be ineffective if you do not then complete the job by producing a sound and effective throughswing. Again, we must come back to the basic principle of the swing. The body has to turn on through to face the target, while the arms swing down and then up again. So, once more, it is a question of turning the body and lifting the arms. The smoothness with which you combine these movements will largely dictate the effectiveness of the swing.

Rather than look at a sequence of pictures as though they represented set stages through which the swing travels, it is more beneficial to isolate the action of the body right through the swing and then to look at the arm action with which it is combined.

The leg and body action has to be initiated with a transference of weight in the left foot and a resultant pull back with the left leg (figs. 28 and 29). In the backswing, I explained how the weight in the left foot moves from being flat on the foot to being on the ball of the foot. The weight should not roll inwards. In the downswing the opposite transference takes place. Weight must now be pushed from the ball of the foot, back onto the left heel. Again, it is a forwards and backwards movement and *not* a sideways movement. The golfer who lets the left heel come off the ground in the backswing will simply feel that she then has to push it back down again in the start of the throughswing. The player whose heel stays down throughout the backswing may have to make a more conscious effort to thrust the pressure back onto the heel.

The weight transference back onto the left heel is important, for it starts the left leg and hip in motion. Through the rest of the swing the left knee should pull itself back under the body, so that it is virtually braced through impact, and continue this pull back so that, by the end of the follow-through, the hips are facing directly towards the target (figs. 30 to 34). At the end of the full swing, the left leg should be reasonably straight, or even braced, but with the left hip pushing out to the side so that you have the feeling of sinking into the left leg and not being stretched up on it (fig. 34).

53

Fig. 28 At the top
of the backswing
the left side is firmly
in control

To enable the body to unwind in this way, it is vital to give it sufficient freedom by moving well with the right foot and leg. At the top of the backswing, the right hip will be turned slightly to the right, with the leg reasonably straight, though never locked. In the throughswing, it is essential for the right foot to spin onto the toes so that, in the end of the swing, the right foot is completely on the tips of the toes, with the sole of the foot facing directly away from the target (figs. 28 to 34). This is absolutely essential, for it enables the hips to turn on through to face the target quite simply at the end of the follow-through. The majority of club golfers never get off the right foot in

Fig. 29 Starting
the downswing
with a pull of the
left arm

the throughswing. Instead, they are very slow to spin onto the toes and usually produce an unfinished swing, where the right foot is trapped and the hips are unable to turn through to face the target. As a rule, if this happens, the player is forced to use too much shoulder action in the throughswing because she is failing to use the lower half of the body, with the result that the top and bottom halves fight against each other and produce general inconsistency. It is essential to get this spinning action with the right foot – hips to the target in the follow-through, sole of the shoe directly away from it.

Fig. 30   The left arm is still in control; the angle in the wrists
is maintained

Fig. 31 Left heel on the ground through impact, wrists released

Fig. 32 Eyes still down, left arm starting to fold away

Fig. 33 Left leg firm, right foot spinning through, head still

Fig. 34 Finish of the swing, clubshaft resting on the shoulder blade

The arm action

While the body and legs are turning on through to the target, the arms have to swing the club down to the ball and then up and through as the swing is completed. At the top of the backswing, the left arm is very much in control and it should remain so for the first part of the downswing (figs. 28 to 30). The changes of direction should be initiated very much with the left hand, having the feeling of pulling the club down several inches with the left hand before the right comes into its own and delivers power to the shot. The right hand and arm are in a potentially very strong position at the top of the backswing, so that it is all too easy to swing round on the shot with the right side dominant – thus losing the correct line to the swing. The good player's swing always shows the left hand very much in control halfway down the downswing. This means that the right hand is still hinged back on itself as it was at the top of the backswing, with the clubhead noticeably behind the hands (fig. 35). The right hand is now ready to throw the clubhead round and into the ball from inside

Fig. 35 Correct: approaching impact with the left side in control

the target line. Maximum speed can be produced, without losing the desired direction of the swing. This should be contrasted to the action of the club player, which usually shows the downswing having been initiated too much with the right arm and hand, so that the right hand is no longer hinged back on itself and the clubhead is level with or even ahead of the hands (fig. 36).

Probably the best exercise to develop this left hand control is simply to swing the club up and down through the top of the backswing and start of the downswing with the left arm alone – just up and down a matter of 18 inches (46 cm).

Once the left hand and arm have initiated the downswing, the right hand unhinges itself and throws the clubhead 'through' the ball. As you reach impact, there is a point at which both arms are straight though still relatively loose and not tense. Just beyond impact, the left arm begins to fold away into the body, just as the right one did in the backswing, while the right arm stays extended to the target until the club approaches waist height (figs. 31 and 32).

Fig. 36 Incorrect: the right side has taken over the downswing

Fig. 37   Incorrect: the left arm is buckling outwards instead of folding inwards

The way in which the left arm is allowed to fold into the body is of utmost importance. I mentioned in the set-up the way in which the left arm should hang – the inside of the arm visible and the elbow joint pointing diagonally downwards. It is in this part of the swing that this left arm position becomes important. The elbow joint should be kept pointing downwards, so that the elbow remains reasonably close to the side as the arm turns (fig. 32). What you must *not* allow to happen is for the left elbow to point directly towards the target and for the arm to break outwards (fig. 37). This is a fairly typical action of the average club golfer – tending to allow the swing to become too narrow through and beyond the ball, so that the direction is lost, while also tending to leave the clubface open at impact, with the result that the ball is sliced away to the right. One of the best exercises to develop the correct folding in of the left arm is to practise swinging the club with the left arm alone, just back and through in the impact area, while keeping hold of the left arm just above the

Fig. 38 Maintaining the target-line at the end of the swing

elbow with the right hand. This will help develop the feeling of keeping the arm folding in correctly, instead of breaking outwards.

As you reach a point at which the club is roughly waist height, there has to be a conscious lifting action in the arms, so that the club is swung up and over the left shoulder to complete the full circle of the swing (figs. 33 and 34). As this happens, the elbows should be kept fairly close together, which keeps the clubhead travelling on the right path. If the elbows can be kept very much together like this, the club travels through to the target and then up and over and away from the target, so that it never really comes off-line. In this way, you have every chance of starting the ball out on target for, really, the club never travels anywhere but on the target-line (fig. 38). By contrast, if the elbows are allowed to separate and spread apart in the throughswing, the clubhead will be pulled off-line and the chances of starting the ball straight are far more remote (fig. 37).

Putting the two together

Ultimately, the effectiveness of the swing depends on the way in which the body action is combined with the arm action. The first point to appreciate is that the shoulders have only to travel a very small distance, while the clubhead has to travel a very long way from the top of the backswing through to the other end of the swing. To achieve a perfect swing, the two have to be synchronised well so that the two movements are completed together. The player who uses her body and shoulders very much faster than her arms and hands is usually prone to slicing; the player whose hands and arms tend to finish their work before the body unwind takes place, is far more likely to have problems with hooking. The greatest problem for the club golfer is, as a rule, to keep the right shoulder in its passive rôle at the change of direction from backswing to downswing. This can be properly corrected only by developing control and power in the left arm, so that it feels strong enough to generate speed without any unwanted assistance from the right side of the body.

Balance

Almost every really good professional golfer displays perfect balance at the end of the follow-through. The club golfer usually assumes that perfect balance should be seen as the result of a good swing, but, in fact, the converse is almost true. Aiming at achieving good balance in the throughswing should be seen as something which *causes* a good swing. With every shot you should work to produce perfect balance at the end of the follow-through, so that the finish is absolutely poised. This serves two very important functions. Firstly, it enables you to check precisely what has happened in the throughswing. Are the elbows together so that the club is pointing directly away from the target-line? Has the right foot spun round correctly onto the end of the toes, with the hips facing towards the target and the left leg firm? This can all be seen from the follow-through.

Secondly, if you can achieve perfect balance in the finish position, it means that the swing has been kept perfectly under control, without the tendency to throw yourself into the shot with too much force.

The practice exercise I always recommend is to hit balls with a medium iron and then gradually work up to a driver, holding the balance in the follow-through until the ball has landed – or for a count of four, whichever is likely to be longer! Almost every great golfer displays perfect balance at the end of the swing; *you* must realise that perfect balance can be the *cause* of a good swing and *not* simply the result of one.

7 From short irons to driver

The basic golfswing – developed with a medium iron – will stand you in good stead for hitting every shot from the short irons to the driver. However, the various shots require slightly different types of contact, so that your concept of the swing has to be altered slightly through the set of clubs. Having mastered a few simple principles, it is then virtually true to say that you should feel the swing is the same for every club; it is just the idea of the contact with the ball which needs adjustment.

The short irons

In hitting good short iron shots – from the 8-iron upwards – you need to achieve maximum accuracy while producing a shot in which the ball stops quickly on landing. Power is *not* all-important. With the short irons, there is usually very little problem in producing a reasonable height to the shot. This means that you can work on producing a solid, repetitive contact with the ball, without having to be too concerned at flighting the ball with sufficient height. To achieve a good, solid contact – taking the ball and then a small divot – the ball should be positioned slightly behind the natural bottom of the swing. This encourages a downward contact (fig. 39). The hands will now be slightly ahead of the ball at address; the farther back in the feet the ball is played, the more the hands will be ahead of it.

Because you are not so much concerned with power as with accuracy, the swing can be slightly shorter than usual, breaking the wrists a little earlier in the swing to create power for the downswing a little sooner. The feeling through impact must then be one of keeping the weight very much ahead of the ball – well on the left foot – while thinking of the descending, ball-turf contact. Although you must still be very conscious of accelerating into the ball, much of the speed and power is taken up with the contact with the turf beyond the ball, so that the finish with these shots is noticeably shorter than with the rest of the full shots. The longer-handicap player should be aware of the feeling of hitting *down* and through the ball, and not of having any temptation to try to lift it into the air. The loft of the club will do that for you. Hit down, watch the ball through impact and the loft of the club will force the ball up (fig. 40).

Fig. 39   The downward attack required for short irons

Fig. 40 The feeling of hitting *down* through impact

However, there is another adjustment which generally needs to be made with the short irons. As you move the ball back in the feet for these shots, in other words towards the right foot, the direction you produce is likely to be altered. The farther towards the right foot the ball is played, the more likely you are to strike it with an 'in-to-out' swing – a swing which is aimed right of target through impact. This is simply because the clubhead has not reached the straight-through part of the swing because it is catching the ball rather earlier. The tendency, if you simply moved the ball back in the feet with no other adjustment, would be to push the ball out to the right of target. What one therefore has to do to compensate for moving the ball back, is to aim the feet slightly left of target – an 'open' stance. The degree to which each individual player has to do this is largely a case of trial and error, but basically, the farther back in the feet the ball is played, the more open the stance will have to be (fig. 41). You must appreciate, however, that the shoulders should, for most players, remain virtually square at address, so that the shoulder line is still on-target and *not* pulled round to the left.

Fig. 41 Setting the feet open to compensate for playing the ball back

Long irons

A problem for most golfers is to achieve a sufficiently good contact with the long irons to produce enough height and carry to the ball. However, once you have mastered the art of using these clubs well, there is hardly a shot more satisfying than a really well-struck 3- or 4-iron.

Personally, I think you need to have two entirely different approaches to long iron shots, depending upon the way in which the ball sits to the ground. If the ball sits up on a slight tuft of grass, or if there is a slight cushion of grass between the ball and ground, the contact with the ball is comparatively easy. In this case, your idea should be that of sweeping the ball fairly cleanly from the top of the grass, striking it right at the bottom of the swing, or even fractionally on the upswing if the ball sits up particularly well. For this type of contact, the ball should be positioned well forward in the feet so that it is likely to coincide with the natural bottom of the swing, or, for the really good lie, is going to be slightly forward of this. You should not, therefore, be thinking of striking the ball with a ball-turf contact, but should be thinking of a nice, clean contact, just clipping the little piece of grass on which the ball sits.

As far as the swing is concerned, the key factor for good long iron play is really maintaining perfect rhythm. The downfall of most golfers is that they press for extra power with long irons. The heads of the club are relatively light and often do not give the impression of power, so that the tendency is to try to force the shot. Added to this, you know that the ball is supposed to fly farther, so that it is all too easy to swing too hard and lose control. With the long irons you need to feel that you are completing *both* ends of the swing, while trying very hard to swing the club with exactly the same timing as with the medium irons. The extra length of shaft gives added speed to the clubhead, without having to strive to achieve it.

From this type of lie – where the ball sits up reasonably well – it should be quite possible to produce plenty of height with the long irons. The player who finds difficulty in achieving sufficient height usually has some kind of problem in the way the hands and wrists work. The first likely cause of trouble is a grip in which the right hand is too much underneath the club, so that the important line between the thumb and index finger points way outside the right shoulder. The right hand is then likely to turn the clubface into a closed position through impact, reducing the effective loft of the club. However, assuming the grip is correct, there are also players who have difficulty in producing the right trajectory through faulty hand action or insufficient hand action. You should very simply feel through impact when extra height is required that the wrists are really loose, so that they swish the ball away. You should, literally, be flicking the ball away with a sudden throwing type of action in the wrists. To produce this, the wrists must stay loose and free. Any kind of tension immobilises them and makes this sudden speed at impact impossible. To produce the correct type of swish with the long irons, the left arm must, in turn, be loose and relaxed so that it can turn and fold into the body (see fig. 32). Whenever people say that 'flicking' the wrists in golf is wrong, what they mean is that the left wrist should not hinge back on itself. I agree that this type of flick is quite wrong. The correct flick of the wrist is simply a matter of staying loose, allowing the left arm, in particular, to stay relaxed so that it can get out of the way of the right, and then developing a throwing action with both hands and wrists so that there is a sudden release of speed and energy through impact.

Long irons – a second approach

In order to play good long irons from comparatively bare or tight lies, a different approach is required. Here the contact required has to be rather more exact, for there is no cushion of grass between the ball and the ground to give any room for error. If the ball sits absolutely tight to the ground, you have either to sweep it away from the top of the ground, with virtually no margin for error, or try to hit the ball with a ball-turf contact, taking a very slight divot beyond it. On the whole, aiming at a perfectly clean contact is usually easier for the really top-class woman golfer, who perhaps lacks quite the strength to take a divot with a 2- or 3-iron. Most top-class male golfers, on the other hand, are usually quite happy to strike long irons from tight lies with a small divot. My advice to the club golfer about which approach to use, would be that the first approach – the one I would use – requires a more perfectly judged contact, while the other requires strength in the hands to keep the light head of a long iron cutting through the turf. If you aim for a perfectly clean contact, the ball should still be positioned to coincide with the exact bottom of your swing. If a small divot is required, the ball can be played a fraction farther to the right in the stance.

The difference between playing this type of long iron shot well and badly is largely a matter of having sufficient nerve and courage. It is very much a question of visualising absolutely perfectly the desired contact, being really single-minded about achieving this contact and then making yourself execute the shot without quitting. Particularly with the 2-iron from a bare lie, it is largely a matter of mustering enough adrenalin at the appropriate moment. But, the first rule is to visualise the contact you want – whether with a divot or not – and then simply to set about achieving it with a perfectly timed swing.

The fairway woods

Fairway woods are really very much like long irons. The difficulty of the shot really depends on the way in which the ball sits. If the lie is good, so that there is half an inch or so of grass between the ball and the ground, the contact is fairly simple and there is half an inch of tolerance in the depth of contact. It does not make much odds whether the bottom of the clubhead comes through exactly level with the bottom of the ball or a quarter of an inch below it. There is enough room for error to give you confidence and the contact really does not have to be too exact.

On the other hand, if there is no grass between the ball and the ground, the contact has to be judged with absolute perfection. The sole of the club has to brush the ground at the very spot on which the ball sits. So, the tighter the lie, the finer the judgement has to be. The swing for both types of lie is really the same; judgement and concentration have to be that bit better from the bare type of lie. However, the problems with fairway woods are not quite what they were with long irons. If the contact is not quite perfect with a fairway wood, the sole of the club will usually slide smoothly along the ground so that the player achieves a virtually faultless shot with a slightly less than perfect contact. With the long iron, on the other hand, the sole of the club will cut into the turf and usually ruin the shot. For this reason, most club golfers will do far better to learn to play really good 4- and 5-wood shots, than to struggle with 2- and even 3-irons.

As far as the swing is concerned with the fairway woods, it is again very much a question of producing a sufficiently full swing – both back and through – maintaining the timing and avoiding any temptation to try to hit the ball too hard. The longer shaft of the woods will produce this extra speed, provided you maintain rhythm. As with the long iron shots, relax and loosen the wrists in order to produce the necessary speed through impact.

The driver

The old cliché is that 'One drives for show and putts for dough'. As far as the world-class professional is concerned, this is almost certainly true, and it is the player who holes the putts who wins the championship. But, for all but the top-class player, there is no doubt that good driving is a great boon. It sets you up for the second shots and takes the pressure off the rest of the game. Any golfer who can hit the fairway with every drive in a round is a long way towards producing a good score – and the woman who can drive consistently is usually in at the kill, even if the putts are not dropping.

With the drive one has to realise that the contact required on the ball is totally different from the contact required with the other clubs. The ball is teed up to help produce maximum flight and carry. To take advantage of this, the ball must be struck with the clubhead travelling upwards, so that the ball is met *after* passing the natural bottom of the swing. To encourage this upward contact, the ball should be positioned well forward in the stance, towards the left foot. This means that the hands may be fractionally behind the clubhead. This does not matter. In turn, the right shoulder will be dropped well below the left, with the left side of the body arched and stretched at address and the right side relaxed and compressed. Thus, in the correct set-up, the right shoulder is very much nearer the right hip than the comparative distance on the left side of the body. This is therefore setting yourself up to be well *behind* the ball, ready to meet it on the upswing (fig. 42).

compressed	stretched

Fig. 42 Producing the correct shallow upward contact for driving

Fig. 43 The body stays well behind the ball with driving; legs are active

The main point to keep in mind is that the attack on the ball must be a shallow, upward one. To help achieve this, the takeaway and first part of the backswing should be kept shallow – with no tendency to lift the club – so that the clubhead is kept low to the ground as it moves away from the club. However, care must be taken to ensure that the clubhead still moves away inside the target-line on a curve. It should never go straight back from the ball or the whole curve of the swing is liable to be lost. The feeling must be one of width and stretch in the left arm, setting you up for the shallow attack on the ball. The rest of the backswing must then show this same width and extension with the left arm, ensuring that the backswing really is completed, so that the important timing at the change of direction in the swing is perfect.

In the downswing, the feeling to be encouraged with the driver, is that of staying very much behind the ball, so that you have the sensation of hitting the ball *away* from you from behind it. It is quite the reverse of the short iron shot, for example, where the feeling can be of being rather ahead of the ball. With the drive, the bottom of the swing is to fall some 8 or 9 inches (20–23 cm) *behind* the ball, so that it is caught on the upswing. For this reason, the whole centre of gravity of the body should be kept opposite this spot – never moving ahead of the ball. In this context, the club golfer has to take great care to ensure that the legs are kept moving in the downswing, while the upper part of the body is kept well back. To produce this, you will often need a definite feeling of arching the body in the downswing, so that the right side is very compressed and the left side is stretched in the impact zone. If you stay correctly behind the ball, and yet use the legs properly, the finish of the swing will see the left leg firm with the right foot having spun through onto the tips of the toes, but, and this is important, with plenty of weight on the big toe of the right foot (fig. 43). With the short and medium irons, the weight distribution in the follow-through may show almost all the weight on the left foot. In the drive, you have to be very conscious, in staying *behind* the ball, of leaving plenty of weight on the *toes* of the right foot. However, in achieving this, the legs must still work really well, so that there is no question of hanging back on the sole of the right foot. The legs must work fast and freely, but with the right side arching and the head staying back through impact to produce this different weight distribution in the finish.

In producing this upward contact on the ball, the feeling should then be one of continuing to swing the club *up* to the target, so that the hands move through a high position, and take the club up and virtually straight back over the left shoulder, into a perfectly balanced position. Great care has to be taken with the driver to see that perfect balance is still produced, with the finish of the swing full and complete, so that the club is right down the back in the follow-through. This helps to ensure that maximum clubhead speed is being maintained through impact, without any loss of balance and control.

Problems with driving

The correct contact with a driver should be totally different from the contact produced with an iron. With the irons, the contact should be a downward or sweeping one depending on the lie. With the driver, the contact must definitely be an *upward* one. Many players find this difficult to achieve. Very often it is simply that they do not realise that the requirement is different and so imagine that exactly the same approach is correct with the driver as with the other clubs. Once you appreciate that the clubhead has to strike the ball in a different way, the task is much easier. The best exercise for encouraging the right attack is to have plenty of practice swings with the driver, looking at the spot where the ball would be but concentrating on brushing the ground some eight to ten inches behind it. The contact with the ground should be as light and shallow as possible, so that when you attempt the same thing with the ball, the club no longer touches the ground, but still attacks the ball in the same shallow arc.

The player who has problems with the driver usually attacks the ball with the club travelling on the downswing instead of on the upswing. Most golfers know the theory that the ball should be played farther towards the left foot with the driver, but fail to understand why this is necessary. Instead of producing a swing where the bottom of it is in the same place as normal, thus striking the ball on the upswing, the club golfer often produces a swing where the bottom of the swing comes right at the ball or certainly much too close to it. One of two things will then happen. Either the clubhead will be tipped over, so that the very top of the head strikes the ball – sending it far too high into the air – or the ball will be driven down far too low and almost into the ground (fig. 44). For good driving, you should feel that the ball is caught with the club moving upwards *from a fairly high tee*. Using a reasonably high tee will encourage you to hit the ball on the upswing. Using too low a tee tends to encourage a wrong, downward contact. The best guide, as far as the tee height is concerned, is to tee the ball so that the top of the clubhead is just above the centre of the ball, which means you can get sufficient height to the shot without danger of the clubhead going right under the ball and so skying it.

◀ Fig. 44 Incorrect: weight ahead of the ball and incorrect downward attack. Most faults with driving come from a faulty downward attack

I am sure every golfer has at some stage thought: 'Ah, at last, I've got it and it isn't going to go wrong again.' But, of course, it does. Golf is a game where adjustment is constantly necessary. For the professional player, whose swing is established and reasonably grooved, there are still small problems which creep in and need ironing out. Very minor changes in the stance or grip, which take place quite subconsciously, can change the whole feel of the swing quite dramatically. The top-class professional can go out on the course with a swing which *looks* precisely the same every day, and yet which feels perfectly comfortable on one day but totally wrong the next. To the onlooker, even with a very trained eye, nothing seems to be different. It is simply a question of feel. So, whatever your standard, do not be surprised if the swing does seem different from one day to another. It always will. Much of the good golfer's work at maintaining her standard is simply a question of feeling comfortable, and very often all she is aiming to do on the practice ground before a round, is to get used to the feeling of the swing she has woken up with that morning. It will look the same, but will not necessarily feel the same.

Much the same is true of the club golfer. One day she has the right feel and the next day she has not. 'Should I do this, or should I do this?' she will say to the professional – producing two swings which to all intents and purposes are identical, yet which may feel dramatically different. So, very largely, what you have to work at is comfort, combined with a correct or, at least, an acceptable technique. You must, therefore, be prepared to experiment, within certain limits, to produce a comfortable, relaxed feeling to the swing, without experimenting to the point where you are changing your whole technique. For example, supposing I stand to the ball in the position which I know and feel to be correct, and then turn my left foot out fractionally, so that the toes move perhaps half an inch – it will feel diabolical. Similarly, if I push my weight fractionally back on my heels or forward on my toes, the whole sensation of the set-up may be ruined. This type of minor adjustment – half an inch here and half an inch there – has to go on continuously, in search of feel. The danger is of overdoing these tiny adjustments to the point where you start tinkering around with the swing and so alter the basic technique. So, really, what I think you must do is to think in terms of two distinct types of change to the swing, which I would term 'alterations' and 'adjustments'. An adjustment, to my mind, is something which does not produce a noticeable change visibly – or certainly not to any but the most trained eye. It does not actually change the whole technique. If I simply turn my left foot in fractionally, or take the club away a degree farther on the inside, these should be adjustments which I can do very simply to keep my game finely tuned. This type of adjustment, even in the 'perfect' golfswing is constantly needed.

On the other hand, if an alteration is to be made, this is something which I would view as changing the whole technique of the swing and this will produce an awkward feeling. When an alteration is being made, there is bound to be some slight lowering of performance at first – whether for 10 shots or 10 rounds – while the alteration is becoming comfortable. With a minor adjustment, there should be no really awkward stage.

So, when trying to improve your own game, be clear as to whether all you need is a slight adjustment – which everyone has to make from time to time – or whether you are trying to alter the whole swing. If the professional tries to alter something in your swing, is she suggesting a real alteration or is she simply helping you to make some very minor adjustment? The simple philosophy is – be prepared to experiment, but avoid too many needless alterations. If the swing begins to feel uncomfortable, be prepared to try standing a little closer or a little farther away, adjust your weight distribution very fractionally or position yourself so that the ball is slightly farther towards one foot or the other. All you are really searching for is feel and there may be little rhyme or reason to explain the minor adjustment you have to make from day to day. Just accept that golf is a game of constant adjustment.

Correcting a faulty shot

For the player who is producing a definite pattern of faulty shots, the problem is rather different from that of the player who is simply making adjustments for a better feel to the swing. The problem for many golfers is that they really do not understand what causes bad shots, so that all they can do is listen to advice or try to sort themselves out through a disastrous process of trial and error. In teaching, I have often come across a situation where a player hits a shot which slices away to the right and then proceeds to hit three or more which do precisely the same. If the professional asks the pupil what *caused* the slice, the answer will usually be something like 'I bent my left arm' or 'I didn't follow through'. Indirectly, either of these faulty actions in the swing *could* cause the poor flight. What the pupil does not usually do, is to point to the problem *with the contact with the ball*. This must be the first stage in any correction at golf: 'What has happened in the contact with the ball?'

The process through which you must go in analysing your own golf – or anyone else's – is this. Firstly, look at the flight of the ball and describe it to yourself. Has the ball flown straight right, or started left and bent to the right, or started to the right and curved farther to the right? So, firstly, analyse the flight of the ball accurately. Secondly, go through the process of thinking what caused this *at impact*. This is the part which club golfers usually miss out or fail to understand. You have to ask yourself, 'How has the clubhead struck the ball to cause this flight?' Then, thirdly, having worked through the other two stages, you can, with experience, begin to think of the likely causes in the swing which are producing this faulty pattern at impact.

Thus, the process of correction should be:

1   Analyse the *flight* of the ball
2   From this analyse the *contact*
3   Pick out the likely cause or causes in the *swing*.

In this way, you are following a logical process, rather than simply trying to correct faults through trial and error or superstitions.

As a rule, the reason why the club golfer is unable to make improvements on her own is that she simply fails to understand what is happening with the contact with the ball – a point I raised in the first chapter. This is crucial to improvement at golf. All good golf teaching must give the pupil an explanation in terms of cause and effect. Initially, the teacher must do the analysis for the pupil. 'This is the flight of shots you are producing. This is caused by such-and-such a pattern at impact. This incorrect contact is being produced either by this or that in the swing. Therefore, this is the adjustment we are going to make.' What the teacher should *not* do is simply point to the incorrect flight and then make an alteration to the swing without explanation. This is quite worthless and really leaves the player no wiser about her swing.

The player who is really well taught will begin to understand the game properly. When the professional then asks her what was wrong with the shot, she begins to give a logical answer – 'Oh, yes, I must have had the clubface open at impact.' Player and teacher can then work together and discuss what probably caused this in the swing. The player begins to think logically and can make well-thought-out corrections. I suppose a professional has a feeling of achievement when a pupil, phoning to make an appointment, describes what is happening to the flight of the shots, instead of complaining about a bent left arm, and has obviously worked out in her mind what is producing this at impact. Very often, I find I can describe the likely changes necessary for the pupil and suggest she works on two or three points until the lesson. Improvement at golf is very logical – once you *understand* the basic principles. So, let us look at these in some depth.

Starting the ball on-target

The first stage in our correction process is analysing the flight of the ball. The club golfer tends to think simply of where the ball finished. This is wrong. You must be clear *how* the ball is travelling. Thus, a ball which finishes 20 yards (18 m) right of target may have flown straight there, or started left of target and bent severely to the right. It may have started fractionally right and bent further right or it may even have started well out to the right and bent to the left at the end. Each of these shots may have finished in virtually the same place, but the contact with the ball for each will have been entirely different and the swing, too, will have differed considerably.

There are, therefore, two distinct elements to the flight of the ball – 'where did it start?' and 'how did it curve?' Let us look at the first of these – our aim being to start the ball on-target.

The basic rule is this: assuming the ball is struck from the middle, or approximately the middle, of the clubface, it will start in the direction in which the swing is travelling. If the ball starts to the left of target, it means the swing was left-aimed through impact. If the ball starts to the right, it means the swing was right-aimed. In order, therefore, to start the ball on-target we want the swing to be travelling on-target through impact.

The shot which starts left

If the tendency is to *start* the ball left of target, there are a number of likely causes. The player gradually begins to know which is the most likely cause in her own swing and can work systematically through the alternatives. These are the possible causes:

1 The player may simply be aiming left of target with either her feet, her shoulders, or with both. This means that the whole line of the swing is left-aimed. This is likely to be caused either by a fear of slicing to the right or from unconscious poor alignment – perhaps a matter of eyesight, with one eye being slightly dominant.

2 The ball may be positioned too far towards the left foot, so that it is being struck *after* the straight-through part of the swing has been passed. Playing the ball too far forward also tends to bring the shoulders into a left-aimed position, so that the two things are inclined to go together (fig. 45).

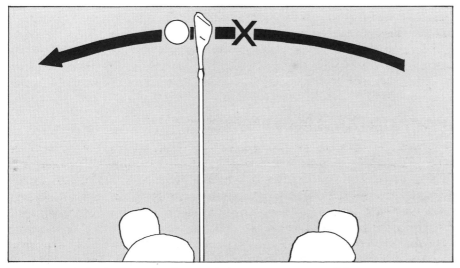

Fig. 45 With the ball too far forward, the impact is now off-line

3   The player may be turning insufficiently in the backswing, so that the line of the club at the top of the backswing is left-aimed and the downswing follows this direction.

4   The player may need to take the club back slightly more on the inside of the target-line in the takeaway, which is likely, in turn, to produce a swing which is aimed a little farther right through impact. The more the club is taken away on the inside, the more likely you are to hit the ball with a right-aimed swing. In other words, the less likely you are to start it left.

5   The player may be very 'right-side dominant' so that the body turns through impact into a left-aimed position. In this case, the correction on a short term basis has to be one of thinking very hard through impact of the desired direction of attack. The long-term improvement has to be the strengthening of the left side.

6   Lastly, the player may simply not be thinking sufficiently strongly about the direction required through impact. She *must* have in mind the direction of the clubhead through impact, so that she draws a mental line out beyond the ball to the target and tries to start the ball out on this line. A very good exercise here is to put a tee or small coin 18 inches (46 cm) ahead of the ball, and then to concentrate on hitting the ball out over this spot.

So, if the ball starts left of target, regardless of where it finishes, one of these faults is present in the swing.

The shot which starts right

The player who produces shots which start out to the right of target, yet come off the middle of the clubface, is striking the ball with a swing which is right-aimed through impact. Again, there are a number of set patterns in the swing that are responsible:

1   The player may simply be aiming to the right with her feet or shoulders. This is a very common fault and is largely caused by a visual distortion in lining up. It is not always easy to see a straight line from the ball to the target and then to stand parallel to this line when the eyes are not directly over the ball-target line. The remedy here is usually to choose a spot on the ground some 15 inches (38 cm) ahead of the ball, on line with the target, and then to concentrate on aiming out over this spot.

2   The ball may be too much towards the right foot, so that it is being struck before the clubhead has reached the straight-through part of the swing. The farther back in the feet the ball is played, the more likely you are to strike it with an 'in-to-out' – in other words, right-aimed – swing.

3   A very common cause of blocking shots out to the right is that the left side of the body does not unwind correctly through impact. As the arms swing down into the ball the body must turn on through so that the hips are completely facing the target at the end of the swing. However, players often produce insufficient legwork in the throughswing and fail to get through onto the toes of the right foot, with the result that the hips are left

facing out to the right at the end of the swing (fig. 46). The problem often comes from the left leg and incorrect weight transference. The correct thing is that the weight in the left foot should be pulled back onto the left heel in the downswing, pulling the left knee back and turning the left hip out of the way. To do this correctly, there should be quite a twist in the left leg. So, if your shots tend to start out to the right of target, check on which direction you face at the finish of the swing.

4 The player who starts the ball right of target may very simply have lost her idea of the direction through impact, so that she is attacking the ball fractionally off-line. This fault is most common to low-handicap players. In this case, all you really have to do is to concentrate on a spot just ahead of the ball and to work at starting the ball out over this spot, instead of letting it start away to the right.

Shots which curve to the left – the hook

We now come to the second element in direction which is that of keeping the ball flying straight. I said in the first chapter that golf is basically a game of spin and curves, and that it is essential for the golfer who wishes to improve to understand why the ball does not fly straight very easily. Of the two shots, hooking and slicing, the hook – where the ball curves to the left – is frequently caused by a swing which is very nearly correct and is usually the easier to correct. The slice, by contrast, is often comparatively hard to correct and is far more the problem of the higher-handicap player and beginner.

The basic principle to understand about the hooked shot is that the clubface is 'closed' to the direction of the swing through impact. In other words, the clubface looks to the left of the line of the swing (fig. 2). This means that the ball is not struck exactly at its back but that the clubface meets it just right of centre, putting on the unwanted sidespin. So, regardless of which way the ball starts – whether to right or left – if it then bends to the left in the air, the clubface was aimed left of this direction of swing. For the player who plays one of the racquet games well, or who plays table tennis, the feeling of a hooked shot is very much like that of a forehand overspin shot, and is produced by much the same action.

The player who produces shots which bend to the left should work systematically through the following checkpoints.

1 Probably 90 per cent of all hooked shots are caused by a fault in the grip and the player who hooks will usually have to look only to her grip to correct the problem. For this reason, the hook is much easier to correct than the slice, which can be produced in many ways. The player who hooks the ball invariably has a 'strong' grip. In this, the left hand is unsuitably on top of the club so that three or four knuckles of the hand show, or the right hand is unsuitably under the club, so that the V between thumb and index finger points out beyond the right shoulder instead of directly to it, or just inside it. Frequently, the player has a combination of

Fig. 46 Inadequate footwork, leaving the body blocked to the right of the target

the two faults, and both hands are wrongly positioned (fig. 9). As the club is returned to impact, the hands turn into a position where the right hand is behind the club and not underneath it, so that the clubhead is turned into a closed position (fig. 10). This immediately puts on hook-spin, and the ball curves away to the left. To correct this, you must have a sensation of keeping the club very much in the fingers of the right hand, so that the hand is right behind the club and not underneath it. The problem for most golfers who hook is that the incorrect grip usually feels much better and more powerful, and the adjustment into the correct grip feels awkward and comparatively weak to start with. In all cases where a grip adjustment like this is made, great care has to be taken not to shift the hands just before the takeaway, but to set the hands in the correct position and then to keep them there.

2 It is, however, quite possible to produce a very closed clubface at impact from a perfect grip – though it is comparatively rare. In this case the player may be closing the clubface by rolling the wrists over too much through impact, so that the back of the left hand faces the ground just beyond impact and the palm of the right hand faces downwards. If this happens, the player will, in turn, produce a very flat, round-the-body follow-through and then simply smother the shot so that it hooks violently to the left. If this happens from a good grip, the player has to work at the feeling of holding the clubface square through impact, so that the clubface is kept travelling up to the target beyond impact instead of being allowed to turn over. Probably the most helpful thought for the player with this type of 'duck hook' is to concentrate on keeping the clubface square at the contact and then to work at good height in the follow-through, so that the arms travel out beyond impact, and are then consciously lifted, instead of being allowed to turn round the body (fig. 47). For this player, it is very important to visualise the clubhead path beyond impact.

3 In some cases, a golfer will still hook the ball from a sound grip because of weakness in the left arm and hand and a very dominant right side. This is often quite common amongst golfers who are good tennis or squash players. The problem here is that the left hand is unable to stand up to the strength and speed of the right, so that the right hand turns the club over through impact, producing the closed clubface. The simple remedy here – and it does not take long – is to work at strengthening the left arm and hand by swinging the club with the left hand alone. I would suggest that any golfer who is right-side dominant swings the club with the left arm alone 30 times a day. After as little as a week there is likely to be a very noticeable difference, but if the left side can be gradually built up to be as strong and active as the right, and then maintained, you have found one of the keys to good golf. A word of warning here. Do ensure that the left arm swings correctly. Start with the left thumb down the front of the club to give support but, most importantly, make sure that the arm swings into a right-angle position at the end of the swing. That is what should happen in

Fig. 47   Remedying the duck hook with a conscious 'lifting' after impact

the full swing. Many players practise this quite incorrectly, leaving the left arm straight at the end of the swing. Firstly, that is not what should happen in the full swing and secondly, it can damage the left shoulder.

4   A shot which curves very slightly to the left can be caused quite simply by some form of misalignment at address. To produce a very slight 'draw', like this, all that is needed is for the clubface and direction of swing to be fractionally at odds with one another, so that the clubface is left of the direction of the set-up. This can be produced either by the clubface aiming a little left, or by the feet, and therefore the swing, aiming fractionally right – the closed stance (fig. 48). In either case, you are set-up to produce some kind of sidespin to the ball. This, in fact, is the way in which the professional golfer usually stands whenever she wants to produce a draw on the ball, so that it curves in smoothly from the right.

Lastly, let me emphasise once again, that almost all hooked shots are caused by a faulty grip and you should *always* experiment at bringing the Vs between thumbs and index fingers closer to the chin before attempting to correct the faulty flight in any other way.

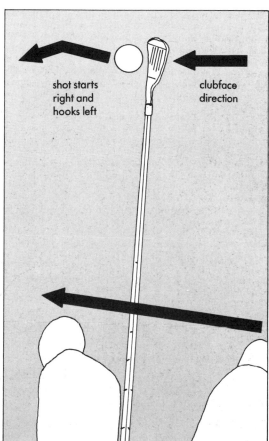

shot starts
right and
hooks left

clubface
direction

Fig. 48 The closed stance.
The line of swing and
clubface converge

Shots which curve to the right

The average club golfer is very much more likely to have problems with slicing the ball than with hooking it. The shot which slices away to the right is caused by an 'open' clubface through impact – in other words, one which looks away to the right of the direction of the swing (fig. 3). The problem is that the player produces insufficient speed in the hands to square up the clubface. There are a number of ways in which faulty hand action is caused.

1   The player may start with a faulty grip. In this case, she adopts a weak grip, in which the lines between the thumbs and index fingers of either or both hands point too near the chin or even left of it, instead of to the right shoulder (fig. 11). As the hands return to impact, the right hand is now behind the club, so that the clubface is returned to the ball in an open position (fig. 12). A faulty left-hand grip is very common to beginners; a faulty right-hand grip is more likely to show up in the good player who has at some stage had to cure a hook and has over-compensated.

2   The player may be far too tense in the wrists and arms, so that the hands are unable to deliver the right kind of throwing action through impact. In golf, the wrists must stay *very, very* loose, and the left arm, in particular, must be perfectly relaxed through impact. The golfer who slices is almost always too stiff and tense; the golfer who hooks is, if anything, too loose. As the clubhead approaches the ball, the hands and wrists must be free enough to swish the clubhead through. Any kind of tension and apprehension will immediately inhibit the correct throwing action. So, relax and loosen up, and do not attempt to steer the ball. Swing freely.

3   A golfer is often unable to square the clubface up through impact because the left arm remains much too rigid through impact and does not fold away as it should. The left arm should be allowed to fold away into the body on the throughswing, just as the right arm did in the backswing. There is a right and a wrong way in which this should happen. The club golfer who slices usually has the left elbow pointing to the target at impact so that the arm breaks outwards in quite the wrong way (fig. 49). This means that the left wrist folds back on itself and the clubface is held open. Instead, the left arm should turn smoothly through impact, so that the elbow begins to point downwards. The elbow then stays fairly close to the body so that the arm folds away smoothly inwards and the clubface can come through squarely (fig. 50).

4   Any tendency to set the clubface open at address will in turn produce an open clubface through impact.

5   A very common cause of leaving the clubface open at impact, particularly with woods, is the use of clubs which are either too heavy or too stiff. A change of driver can rectify this problem quite simply.

The most common problems for the slicer are almost always tension, which inhibits the correct wrist action, or a left arm which produces a blocking action through impact instead of getting itself out of the way.

Fig. 49 Incorrect: the typical slice position at impact – the left arm is buckling outwards and the clubface is open

Fig. 50 Correct: the left arm is folding inwards and the toe of the club
is pointing upwards

Added problems for the slicer

The trouble with slicing is that the golfer usually starts trying to correct the fault without professional advice and in doing so makes the problem worse. She sees the ball curve away to the right of target every time. Therefore she starts to aim or swing to the left in an attempt to hit the ball on-target. However, the direction of the swing and clubface are then aimed more and more across each other. By this time the player is cutting across the ball, so that she imparts even greater sidespin, just like a cut shot at tennis or table tennis. The more she swings to the left, the more the clubface cuts across the ball and so the worse the slice-spin becomes. The classic slice of the club golfer is therefore a shot which starts left of target – the direction of the swing – but which then curves back and away to the right, caused by the poor hand action. The difficulty in correcting this shot is that it is very hard to make yourself attack the ball with a swing which is not left-aimed when you see the ball curving away to the right all the time. Instinctively you swing to the left and who can blame you?

I tackle the pupil's slice by firstly trying to produce the correct hand action, either by changing the grip or by encouraging the correct type of looseness. My aim, then, is to get the player to hit the ball straight left – in other words, to work with her wrongly aimed swing, but simply to try to eliminate the bend in the shot. When I can get her to hit the ball without a curve, it is then much easier to sort out the line of the swing. If she begins to feel that the ball will fly left of target we can tackle the line of the swing and so get the ball flying on-target.

So, my key points for the slicer are to relax and generally loosen the wrists, swish the clubhead through the ball and, if necessary, adapt the grip until the ball can be made to curve to the left. Then tackle the direction of the swing. The chief rule is relaxation.

Producing a solid contact

The advice I have given so far on correcting faults in the flight of shots assumes that the ball is being struck from the middle of the clubhead. However, very many golfers produce bad shots because the ball is not being struck fairly and squarely in the middle of the clubface. The problem for most of these golfers is that they simply do not understand what is happening. They try to make a correction without knowing what they are trying to correct.

If the ball is being struck near the end of the toe of the club, the contact with the ball will feel weak and there may be some tendency to hit shots which push away slightly right of target. If the ball shoots out to the right quite dramatically it has probably been caught off the very end of the club. This is either caused by standing too far from the ball, or by not swinging down in the right place. After all, you have only to be an inch out at impact for the ball not to come from the centre of the club.

Fig. 51   The incorrect address and contact which produces a socket

The problem for the inexperienced player is usually to determine whether a shot which shoots out to the right has come from the toe in this way, or from the socket. The socket, or shank, with the iron is a shot which comes off the very bottom of the shaft (fig. 51). If the ball is struck from this part of the clubhead, it will also shoot out to the right. Any good player suddenly producing this kind of shot would instinctively know from the feel which part of the club it had come from. A player who does not know which shot she is producing has very little chance of correcting the fault. Let us look at the remedies. The first practice technique is to put a blob of lipstick or chalk on the back of the ball and then see where it leaves a mark on the clubface. If the ball is struck from the toe of the club, the solution is usually to stand in closer to it or to stretch out more through impact. If the tendency is to strike the ball off the heel, then you should practise hitting the ball with another ball about an inch away, just outside the first (fig. 52).

Fig. 52 The practice technique for remedying a socket, hitting the inside ball

Then you should concentrate on striking the inside ball without hitting the outside one as well. If you tend to shank you will find yourself making contact with both balls at the same time. The shank can be caused by many different problems in the swing, but what tends to be overlooked as far as the contact is concerned, is that you are simply coming down outside the spot where you started. All you need to do is to work at striking the ball nearer the toe of the club.

I would suggest to any golfer that she should periodically check whether or not she is striking the ball with the middle of the clubface – the best check simply being that of using the chalk or lipstick test. Frequently, comparatively good golfers are found to be striking the ball slightly away from the centre of the club, without knowing it. The problem can get worse until serious faults arise.

Topping the ball

Many golfers find initial problems in brushing the ground as they strike the ball. Instead the clubhead tends to catch the ball around its middle or on its top, so that it simply runs along the ground, instead of flying through the air. There are three common reasons for this trouble:

1   A player may simply be inexperienced and untrained in the idea of brushing the ground. I would suggest here that the golfer should have plenty of practice swings, concentrating on brushing the ground with each swing. In trying the same thing with the ball you must be very conscious of watching the *back* of the ball and not the top of it. If you look at the top of the ball, or move your eyes to the top of it in the swing, that is the part of the ball you are likely to hit.

2   A second common cause of topped shots is that the player tries to lift the ball, instead of simply brushing the ground. In an attempt to lift the ball, the golfer often falls back onto the right foot, feeling that in so doing she can in some way get under the ball (fig. 53). In fact, the club brushes the ground behind the ball and is actually being lifted as it comes through impact, so that it strikes the ball on the top instead of beneath it. The thought one should have in order to correct this is of pushing the weight very firmly back onto the left foot and of hitting *down* into the ball, rather than of trying to lift it. Do remember that a golf ball sits on the ground so that you cannot get under it. Golf is not like other ball games where the ball is usually struck in mid-air and so can be hit from underneath. In golf, the aim should be to brush the ground beneath the ball, and not to try to lift the ball.

3   The golfer who produces the occasional topped or thin shot is usually guilty only of tightening up instead of maintaining the correct relaxation. As she tightens up, her body is pulled up and the radius of her swing is shortened, so that the club no longer reaches the ground through impact. For the golfer who tends to thin the ball under pressure I would stress the importance of staying as relaxed as possible and also of watching the ball really well through impact.

Skied drives

The golfer in the medium-handicap range usually learns to hit good, solid iron shots with a nice divot, but then begins to lose the correct contact with her driver. As a rule the player has mastered the idea of hitting iron shots with a descending blow, but then begins to hit drives in the same way, instead of catching them on the upswing as she should. With the driver, the idea is that the bottom of the swing should fall some eight or ten inches behind the ball, striking it on the upswing. The golfer who skies her drives usually brings the bottom of the swing right to the ball, so that the ball is struck from the top of the clubhead. This type of player will usually in fact hit much better shots with the fairway woods than she will with the driver. The emphasis here must be on setting up well behind the ball, so that the right side of the body is compressed and the left side stretched. In the swing, the legs must be active, but the centre of gravity of the body should stay well behind the ball so that the feeling is one of arching the body and striking the ball on the upswing (fig. 43). In the practice swing, the player should look at the spot where the ball would be, but should work hard at producing a shallow contact, where the clubhead brushes the ground some eight to ten inches behind this spot. The skied drive is basically caused by an unsuitably steep, downward contact, instead of a shallow upward one.

◀ Fig. 53 Incorrect: weight is falling backwards and there is bad upward contact with the ball. Topped shots are produced by trying to lift the ball

9 The art of putting

Putting is really a game all of its own. There are good golfers who cannot putt particularly well and club players who are geniuses on the green. Putting is largely a matter of having a good eye for the ball and being able to see the right line and strike the ball along it. The best putters are born with the right kind of vision and often have styles all of their own which would not work for the ordinary mortal. However, with practice and a good technique, there is little reason why most club golfers should not learn to putt as well as the average tournament golfer. For the high-handicap player, improvement at putting is usually very much easier and quicker than improvement at other parts of the game, and can bring about quite dramatic reductions in her overall score fairly easily.

Putting grips

It is perfectly acceptable to use the ordinary golf grip for putting. In fact, it is perfectly acceptable to use any grip which works effectively. However, the majority of good golfers adapt the ordinary golf grip very slightly for putting. The most usually adopted grip is the 'reverse overlapping grip'. In this, the hands are in the same basic position as for the Vardon grip, except that the palms of the hands are rather more to the sides of the club, instead of having the left one slightly on top and the right one slightly beneath. This helps to keep the clubhead square to the hole. The thumbs are then more or less on the front of the grip. However, the main change is that the left index finger is the one which is on the outside of the grip, covering the little finger of the right hand, or spread right down the outside of the other fingers of the right hand (fig. 54).

The object of doing this is to put the index finger of the left hand into a position where it is very much in control in the backswing, and can easily push the putter head back on line.

An additional or alternative adjustment which many players use, is to extend the right index finger down the shaft of the club, so that it is directly behind the shaft. The reason for doing this is that it sometimes gives the player a better feel for pushing the putter through to the hole at impact and beyond.

Whether or not either or both of these adaptations is made, the basic principle about every good putting grip is that the palms of the hands should be kept to the *sides* of the putter shaft, with the thumbs on top.

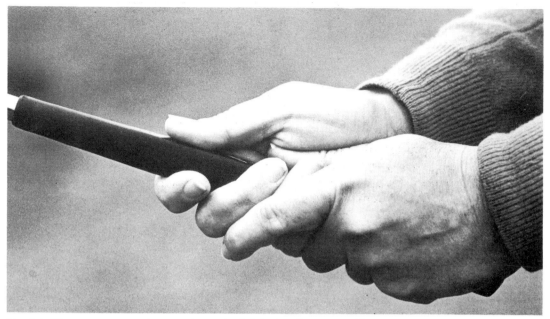

Fig. 54 The reverse overlap putting grip, left index finger outside

The stance

The putting stance is very largely a matter of individual comfort and preference. Some players feel that they have a better view of the hole if they stoop over considerably; others like to stand up at near maximum height. Some putt best from an open stance, others from a closed stance. Many professionals advocate playing the ball from the centre of the stance, others play it well towards the left foot and some to the right. This is all a matter of trial and error and is something with which most players continually experiment, in the search for the perfect position.

However, there are a number of basic rules which almost all professionals agree are fundamental to good putting. The first rule is that the eyes should be directly over the ball, so that it is as easy as possible to judge the straight line from the ball to the target (fig. 55). If anything, it is probably better to err on the side of having the eyes over a spot closer to the feet than outside the ball. This head position is important. If the eyes are over a spot *outside* the ball, you will find that the tendency is usually to pull the ball to the left of the target; conversely, if the eyes are over a spot inside the ball-target line, the tendency is to push the ball to the right of the hole.

The second rule is that the hands should always be level with or slightly ahead of the ball and never behind it. If the hands do tend to get behind the ball at address, it is almost certain that the putter head will start to rise as it strikes the ball and lose the desired solid contact.

Fig. 55   Eyes directly over the ball at address, wrists arched up

Thirdly, the blade of the putter should be absolutely square to the line along which you intend to hit it, with the ball opposite the 'sweet spot' of the club face. The sweet spot is simply the small area near the centre of the face which produces the liveliest and springiest feel. If the ball is played too near the heel, the contact will seem harsh and uncontrolled. If it is played too near the toe, the contact will seem weak and lifeless.

Developing a good stroke

Particularly with short putting, where the direction is absolutely crucial, it is essential to develop a sound stroke, in which the clubhead moves back and through on a straight line through the ball (figs. 55 to 57). For longer putts the stroke needs to become slightly longer, so that the putter has to start moving

Fig. 56 The putter travels back on a straight line, blade below

Fig. 57 The putter must move through on-target; the head should be perfectly still

on a smooth curve. But for the short putt, the prime requirement is for the club to travel along a short, straight line. The easiest way to achieve this is to practise swinging the putter head back and through along a line on a patterned carpet or between two other clubs to produce a kind of track. You can actually develop this stroke by watching the clubhead as it moves back and through, although in executing the putt, your eyes must be firmly focused on the back of the ball.

The problem for most players who have a poor stroke is that the putter head is pulled inside the target-line as the ball is struck and swings in too close to the feet. This has a tendency either to pull the ball left of the hole, or to impart an unwanted sidespin onto it. The trouble is largely caused by the player looking away from the ball too soon, so that the whole shoulder line is turned to the left prematurely. To develop a really good stroke, in which the club does travel through to the hole, it is essential that the eyes should be firmly fixed on the back of the ball, with the head kept perfectly still for a couple of seconds after impact. If you can achieve this in practice, it gives a little room for looking up fractionally earlier when under pressure on the course. In their anxiety, it is the tendency of almost all golfers – amateur and professional – to look up a split second too soon. A very good rule is simply to stay right down on short putts until you *hear* the ball drop in the hole – or, at least, until you are sure it has missed! In doing this, you will also soon see if the clubhead is being pulled away off-line and so be able to correct the fault more easily.

Another very good tip, which is aimed at doing much the same thing – training you to watch the ball and to keep the club moving on line – is to concentrate on swinging the putter head back, through and then returning it to address after the ball has been struck. In this way, your eyes are kept down for a moment after impact, and it becomes obvious if the clubhead has deviated from its correct path.

Choosing the right line

Besides a good stroke with short putting, it is essential to be able to select the right line to allow for any slope of the ground and then to be able to hit the ball along this line. Reading the greens well is largely a matter of experience and there is really no other way of learning this skill than through practice and play. However, there are a number of points which may help you to acquire this skill as quickly as possible. Firstly, you have to bear in mind that the ball turns off-line most towards the end of its run. This is when the ball is losing speed and the slope has most effect. Secondly, the ball will tend to curve away more on a fast green than it will where the green is damp or the grass is thick. In assessing the degree of the slope you may find it helpful to get an overall impression of the entire contour of the green and surrounding fairway.

Having determined the slope of the ground, you have to make a definite decision about the line on which to strike the ball. For a short putt, there may be two distinct choices. Either you can bang the ball firmly at the hole, in which case it is likely to deviate very little, or you can hit the ball with much less force so that it trickles towards the hole, but swings rather more off-line. The player who is really confident is usually much happier to strike a ball firmly at the back of the hole and tends not to worry about missing the hole and being left with an awkward return putt. The player who lacks confidence usually hits the ball without sufficient authority and then has to allow for much more turn to the putt. Ideally, you should attempt something between the two – a putt which is sufficiently firmly struck for it to hold its line well, but which, if it does miss will not go more than perhaps 18 inches (46 cm) past. When you have decided on the amount of borrow necessary – in other words, the amount you have to allow to the side – it is essential to choose a definite spot to the side of the hole and to concentrate on striking the ball at that spot.

Good long putting

Although the direction is still important with long putts, the main problem is usually to judge distance accurately. It is perhaps true to say that the stroke becomes rather less important and that, instead, you should be concentrating on developing the right feel for distance. With long putting it is essential to have a couple of practice swings which are really rehearsals in your mind for producing the right distance for the putt. It is as well, when you do these practice swings, to look at the hole as you do them, rather than at the ground. Then try to visualise how the ball would be rolling with the strength of stroke you are using. With a particularly long putt, it is often a good idea to walk the length of the shot to try to get a better impression of the real distance. You might also find it helpful to squat down and look at the putt from the side to get a closer view of any up or down slope. To achieve a really good touch with long putting the hands and wrists can be brought into play rather more than with the short putt. However, you must still be very careful to watch the ball right up to the moment of impact and to concentrate on a solid contact at the very back of the ball.

10 Short game techniques

If you are to score well around the golf course, it is essential that you should work at the short game. The difference between the player who has a low handicap and one who is bordering on championship standard is very often simply a matter of a difference in their ability around the greens. Similarly, the easiest way for most long-handicap players to reduce their scores is by working at improving these techniques, rather than simply concentrating on the long game and driving. Because most success with the short game can be put down to lots of practice and experience it is not something the newer golfer can hope to master immediately. It does take time. However, there are definitely right and wrong ways of playing short game shots, and adopting the correct methods will at least give you a far better chance of producing the desired shot.

The two shots used around the green are the chip or 'pitch and run' and the pitch. It is important to distinguish between the two and not to produce a shot which falls half-way between. The chip is a shot which is played with one of the medium irons – the 5, 6 or 7 – where the ball jumps forward a few feet and then runs the rest of the way. It should be a low, running shot. By contrast, the pitch is supposed to carry virtually the whole way to the target, land softly and run only a short distance. To get this maximum height the shot is played with one of the wedges. What you do not want is some kind of shot played with an 8- or 9-iron which you might assume will serve both purposes. The two shots are quite distinct, and any tendency to fall between the two usually spells disaster.

Basic chipping

To become good at chipping – the little running shot – I would suggest that you have to move through three distinct phases as you become more skilful. This basic stage is the way in which I would teach the beginner to approach these little shots. In each case, I recommend the use of either the 6- or 7-iron.

The chip is a little shot, which is lofted a couple of feet in the air and then runs to the target. The simple way to learn it is to think of it as being a putt with a slightly lofted club. If you can grasp this idea, then you are halfway towards playing the shot well. To learn the basic chip, adopt a position that feels rather stiff and wooden with the arms straight, the feet slightly closer together than for the full shots, both feet turned slightly towards the target

Fig. 58 Developing a chipping action: wrists stay firm so that arms and hands swing in one piece; legs move freely

Fig. 59 Incorrect: the left arm has stopped moving through impact

and the weight predominantly on the left foot. The swing should now be equally stiff and slightly wooden, allowing the legs to move freely, but producing the feeling that the swing is largely from the shoulders, with both wrists being kept absolutely solid (figs. 60 to 62). In doing this you should develop the firmness in the wrists which is necessary for chipping (fig. 58).

The most common fault of the beginner in learning to chip is that she lets the left wrist fold up in the throughswing, in an attempt to scoop the ball into the air (fig. 59). This is the biggest hurdle to get over in learning both short game shots, and the reason why a certain amount of stiffness is initially important. The fault here is really that the left hand and arm have stopped

Fig. 60 The chipping address: wrists are high, elbows are in, and the club is slightly on its toe

Fig. 61 Firm wrists in the backswing, weight favouring the left foot

moving through impact, so that the right one flicks past it. The correct sensation must be one of *keeping the left arm moving through impact.*

So, the first stage to good chipping must be to develop firmness in the wrists while letting the legs move reasonably freely.

To vary the length of the shot, you should simply adjust the length of the swing. The shorter the shot you want, the shorter the swing must be; the longer the shot, the longer the swing. The basic problem for most golfers is to swing the club through a short enough distance: they find it hard to swing the club a matter of 18 inches (46 cm) or so on the backswing, and so usually tend

Fig. 62 Just beyond impact; wrists are still firm and elbows are tucked in

to swing much too far back, slowing down into impact. This is quite wrong. The backswing must be short enough so that the club can be kept accelerating through impact. To produce the correct length of swing you should have a couple of practice swings, to rehearse the length, if necessary watching the clubhead both back and through to check the distance being produced. With the ball, you should still be very conscious of the length of the swing, being well aware of where the clubhead is travelling and seeing it out of the corner of the right eye. So, keep the swing short enough and accelerate, rather than swinging too far and slowing down.

More advanced chipping

When you have learnt to produce a solid contact with the chip, the next aim is to produce a much better feel, so that you can begin to judge the shot really well and hope to get it close enough for one putt. The first adjustment to make, if you are a more advanced player, is to relax the arms and soften the leg position, so that the whole set-up looks very much more relaxed. I would suggest bending the knees and even bending the arms, so that you come in closer to the ball and begin to get rather more idea of feel in the head of the club (fig. 60). In this second phase, the swing is really very much the same as for the beginner. Emphasis is on the left wrist staying firm through impact, and the left arm being kept moving, so that the upper half of the body works as a unit, without any independent movement in the wrists. The feeling I like to have with these shots is that all the movement is initiated with the legs, so that it is the leg action which *makes* the arms move. Once again, the swing must be kept short enough, so that you feel that you are able to accelerate through the ball, rather than tending to slow down into it (figs. 61, 62). The more advanced player can begin to develop this softer action and work at producing a little more feel and control for length using a putting grip for chipping (fig. 63).

A good tip I would add at this stage is to work at playing the ball rather more towards the toe of the club than may be the case with the full shots. Very often, if the ball is played well towards the toe of the club, there is a more sensitive feel and you really do have a better sensation of the ball coming off the clubface. If the ball is played too much towards the heel of the club it often springs off with too much force, with the result that you have little control of direction.

The third phase in chipping is the one I teach to the really experienced player who is looking to get the ball close to the hole every time. In this case, for added feel, you can develop the action further so that the short chip is played almost entirely with the hands and fingers. This is *not* for the average club golfer. The technique in this case is to set-up very much as before, with the arms relaxed and the knees bent, but now to allow the wrists too to relax. The shot is then executed almost entirely with the hands and wrists, just concentrating on nipping the little piece of grass on which the ball sits. This is the ultimate method for producing really perfect feel for chipping, and is the one most professionals use. However, it must be emphasised here that the shot has to be executed absolutely perfectly or it is dangerous. For this reason, the professional will often drop back to use the second method I described if she feels her game is not quite up to scratch. If you can eventually learn to use a little hand action for chipping, then there is more chance of becoming exceptionally good at it. However, I must stress that the first priority should be a solid contact, played with firm wrists, before this can be attempted.

Fig. 63 The advanced chipping grip, similar to the putting grip: ▶
thumbs to the front, left elbow in

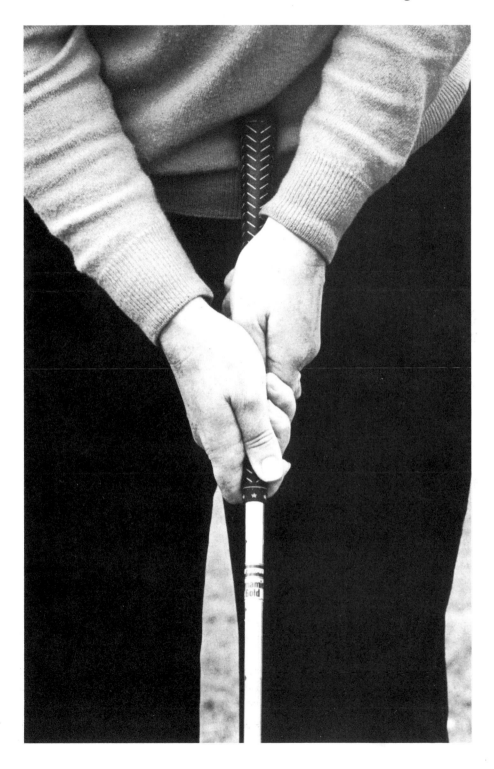

The up-and-over pitch

Whenever I give a clinic on pitching and the short game, I always find a lot of confusion as to how the pitch should be played. Much of the problem is caused by the fact that there are really two different types of pitching shot. There is the little one around the green – the one I call the 'up-and-over' pitch – where all you try to do is to loft the ball a few yards over the bunker. On the other hand, the term 'pitch' also describes a shot of anything up to 100 yards (91 m), played with a wedge or even 9-iron. These two shots require entirely separate techniques. I am sure much of the confusion is caused by players not appreciating that there are these two distinct shots – both with the same name – and so trying to use one method for both shots.

The first shot to look at is the little pitch, which is really a semi-recovery shot around the green. I would play this shot only when there is something to go over, and not from a lie around the green when you could more simply use a

Left: Fig. 64; *right*: Fig. 65

Figs. 64–67 The 'up-and-over' pitch. The weight is set very much on the left foot; arms and wrists are solid

putt or chip. Only pitch if there is something to go over. The club I would always use is a sand iron – the principle being that if you want to get height, use the most lofted club you possess. However, you can use the pitching wedge, though I would hazard a guess that more tournament professionals use a sand iron.

The shot should be executed in much the same way as the basic chipping action. The hands should be a couple of inches down the grip, the arms hanging straight, though reasonably relaxed, but with the left wrist fairly firm. The weight should be very much on the left foot, feet turned towards the target (fig. 64). The action is then predominantly one of moving the legs to make the arms move. This means that the legs turn on the backswing and then turn on through in the throughswing, while the hands stay fairly close to the body (figs. 65 and 66). If this is done correctly, you can see that the end of the shaft hardly moves away from the body and is still being moved as a unit with the arms. If the legs do not move sufficiently, the shaft of the club will be

moved away from the body quite noticeably (fig. 67). So, the emphasis must be on moving the legs to *make* the arms move, and *not* simply pushing the arms back and through from the shoulders.

When you have learnt the basic action with this shot, the most important thought in your mind in playing the shot should be of the contact with the ball. You should be aiming at simply brushing the little piece of ground on which the ball sits. The tighter and barer the lie, the more difficult this is to achieve. Before playing a shot of this kind, you need three or four small practice swings, trying to brush the ground with each and to feel the depth of contact required. If the ball sits on a cushion of grass, the contact is going to be fairly straightforward and there is a small margin for error in the depth of contact. On the other hand, if the lie is completely bare, you have to be extremely accurate in finding the right depth at impact. Whatever the lie, the swing should be precisely the same – concentrating on brushing the grass or scraping the ground as the lie dictates.

As with chipping, the length of the shot is governed by the length of the

Left: Fig. 66; *right*: Fig. 67

swing, keeping both backswing and throughswing to roughly the same length, and ensuring that the backswing is short enough to allow the club to accelerate, rather than decelerate, into the ball.

When you can execute these shots correctly, it becomes most important to judge the exact length of the shot. With chipping, I think of the overall length of the shot and do not try to assess where the ball should land and how much it will then run. With the up-and-over pitch, however, it is vital to choose a spot on the green where you want to land the ball and to assess correctly the amount it will then run. It is often worth walking forward onto the green to judge the length and choose this spot. If you simply look from behind the ball, the distance tends to be foreshortened and distorted and you are liable to select the wrong landing spot. Having chosen this target, it is vital to be able to look down at the ball to execute the shot, but to keep a mental image of where you are trying to land the ball. In throwing a ball you can look at the target; in this kind of golf shot, you need to be very aware of the target but you have to set a correct picture of your target in your mind before trying to play the shot.

Adding height to the pitch

Very occasionally, the ordinary loft of the sand iron is insufficient for the shot required. This problem may arise, for example, if you are faced with a particularly high bunker or steep bank to negotiate. Where it is necessary to produce extra height, the shot should be played with an open clubface. This means that you turn the clubhead slightly, *before* gripping the club, to increase the effective loft of the club (fig. 68). In increasing the loft of the club in this way, the clubface will also turn out to the right very slightly. This may look rather awkward and be slightly off-putting to the inexperienced player but, in fact, it causes very little problem. An ordinary up-and-over pitch can be played with an open clubface without making any other real adjustments. As you become familiar with the shot, you will see that the ball tends to drift away to the right slightly. To counteract this, the feet should be aimed a little left of target – the simplest feeling being that of picking out a target slightly left of the flag, and just allowing for the ball to drift away slightly to the right.

With the clubface opened in this way to produce added height, the length of the swing will have to be increased very slightly to allow for the added loft of the club.

Fig. 68 The open clubface for added height. Aim left to compensate

The long pitch

The longer pitch of, say, 40 to 80 yards (37–73 m), should be played in an entirely different way. I would play these shots with a sand iron up to around 50 yards (46 m) and only then resort to my pitching wedge. Some professionals use a pitching wedge for all such shots. This is largely a matter of personal preference, though I would strongly recommend the average and better than average golfer to experiment with the sand iron, and not simply to think of it as a club for playing from bunkers.

With the longer pitch, the whole contact with the ball is different. The up-and-over pitch is played with a contact which just brushes the grass or scrapes the ground. With this longer shot, the aim must be to strike the ball and then to take a good, solid divot beyond it. To make it as easy as possible to produce this contact, the weight should be set well on the left foot, with the ball quite well back towards the right foot, so that the hands are very noticeably in front of the clubhead (fig. 69). With the ball positioned well back in the stance in this way, the tendency is to hit the ball out to the right. To offset this, the line of the feet should aim to the left of the target – the 'open' stance. The amount you have to turn is largely discovered through trial and error, and varies considerably from one player to another. However, the main point is to realise that some kind of adjustment of this kind is necessary. The last point to mention in the set-up is the angle of the clubface. In moving the ball back in the feet, it is very easy to allow the clubface to be turned into an open position; care should always be taken to ensure that the front of the clubhead is still aimed on-target.

The backswing with these shots is entirely different from the backswing with the up-and-over pitch. With the long pitch, the emphasis in the backswing should be on breaking the wrists early in the swing, so that the takeaway is executed very largely with the hands and wrists (fig. 70). In the short pitch, by contrast, the whole emphasis has to be on keeping the wrists and hands firm. Having literally picked the club up with the hands in the backswing, the main essential of the downswing is to push the weight smartly back onto the left foot, so that the weight of the body is well ahead of the ball at impact (fig. 71). This ensures that the hands are kept in front of the clubhead through impact, producing the necessary downward contact through the ball and turf. As the swing is continued, the action is completely different from a full shot. In the standard full shot the left arm should fold neatly into the body so that the follow-through is long and full. In the long pitch, by contrast, the left arm should stay absolutely firm and braced beyond impact, so that you produce a solid, punchy finish (fig. 72). In this way, the clubhead is kept on-target and the ball travels on-line. This firm, shortened finish is important for good pitching and produces a far more penetrating shot than one produced if the left arm is allowed to fold away just beyond impact.

Finally, you must be conscious in this shot, as in all shots from driver to putting, of watching the ball through impact. There should be a most definite

(Figs. 69–72)   The longer pitch: ball back, hands forward. The club is picked up with an early wrist break, driving down and through the ball, and blocking the swing on a very firm left arm

sensation of watching the ball until it has gone, and then being left looking down at the ground beneath.

The long pitch is a very simple shot to execute, once you have grasped the idea of picking the club up early with the hands in the backswing and yet producing this firm, short follow-through. In fact, it is really the only shot in golf where the backswing and through-swing do not mirror one another. In virtually every other shot the length of the two halves of the swing should be almost identical. Once you can produce these two contrasting halves to the swing, the technique is easy and all you are really concerned with is judging the distance absolutely accurately. In this case, the feel for distance is largely a question of practice and experience for you not only shorten or lengthen the swing but you also adjust the whole speed of the swing to produce a different strength of shot.

A major problem for most players is the shot which falls somewhere in between the two types of pitch – the shot of perhaps 20 to 40 yards (18–37 m). You can either play this length of shot by extending the swing for the up-and-over pitch, or you can try to cut down the action used for the longer

Fig. 71   Fig. 72

pitch. The main point is to decide quite definitely which method is being used and not to fall somewhere between the two. As a general rule, I would suggest that the average club golfer is better, if in doubt, to use the stiffer method of the shorter pitch and to extend this by using more leg action and swinging the arms rather farther. It usually takes a very good player to be able to adapt the hands and wrists method of the longer pitch to the shorter shots. The reason is this. If you use the hands and wrists in the takeaway it is very, very difficult to produce a sufficiently short and delicate backswing to enable you to accelerate through the ball. A club player who tries to use the hands for a relatively short shot usually finds that she produces a much longer swing than she intended, or than is suitable, so that she is forced to slow down and quit on the shot, with disastrous results. Certainly, professionals are to be seen using a delicate hands and wrists action for comparatively short shots, but this is *not* the method for anyone but the really good player. In this matter my guiding rule for the club golfer is to keep the wrist action out of pitching unless it is really essential to achieve sufficient distance.

11 Better bunker play

Many club golfers find bunker shots the most difficult part of the game: yet, for the professional, a shot from a bunker is often almost easier than a comparable shot from grass. These shots are often made difficult for the club player because she does not possess a good sand iron. This club really is an absolute essential for every golfer, for, without it, bunker shots and many other short shots around the green are much more difficult than they need be. Sand irons vary quite considerably. I look for a club with a rounded leading edge and a medium depth of flange at the bottom of the club. As a matter of confidence, a club with a rounded leading edge is psychologically very much easier to use for a variety of shots than one with a straight edge. This is because in many of the sand iron shots you have to open the clubface to increase the effective loft. In doing this, the clubface is also turned away to the right very slightly (fig. 68). As you do this, a club with a very straight leading edge will look to be sitting awkwardly, but a club with a rounded edge will inspire rather greater confidence.

The basic splash shot

The first type of bunker shot to learn is the splash shot, which is played from a bunker close to the green where the ball is sitting well. The idea of this shot, as the name implies, is to splash out a handful of sand, with the ball in the middle of it. You do not actually make contact with the ball – it is simply thrown out with the sand.

In producing this shot, it is very important to adopt the correct set-up. The first point to bear in mind is that the clubhead is going to enter the sand about an inch and a half behind the ball, splash through the sand and then come out of the sand about one and a half inches beyond the original ball position. To make this as easy as possible, the clubhead is positioned over this entry spot in the sand behind the ball, with the eyes focused on the spot in the sand and *not* on the ball. The clubhead should be as close to the sand as possible, without touching it, with the weight concentrated slightly on the left foot and the stance opened towards the target (fig. 73).

The swing with a basic splash shot must be full and very, very slow. The essential point in the backswing is to ensure that the eyes are still kept focused on the spot in the sand *behind* the ball, and not on the ball itself. The club is then almost lifted up in the backswing to produce a steep, U-shaped swing,

Fig. 73 The splash shot, clubface open 1½ inches (4 cm) behind the ball

Fig. 74 The wristbreak is early and free; weight is on the left foot

Fig. 75 The throughswing is slow and
continuous, splashing through the sand

Fig. 76 The follow-through is full, although
the swing is slow

almost letting the left arm relax slightly to develop the right kind of steepness (fig. 74). Throughout the backswing, the weight should be kept slightly more towards the left foot than it would be in the ordinary full shot from the fairway.

As the downswing takes place it is essential to keep the eyes on the spot in the sand while swinging *through* the sand and out the other side, with a really smooth, slow action. Your whole idea of the contact must be one of splashing the sand out – not stabbing into it or chopping at the ball. In fact, you will find that the slower your swing is through the sand, the more easily the club will penetrate it. If you chop at the ball, the sand puts up much more resistance, becomes compacted and you finish up with the clubhead being trapped. Remember – the aim should be to splash into the sand behind the ball and out of the sand beyond it (fig. 75).

In order to keep the clubhead penetrating through the sand, a good bunker player almost always has a really long, relaxed follow-through (fig. 76). Thinking of swinging the club through in this way ensures that speed is not lost at or before the ball. The whole essence of good bunker shots is a slow, full, U-shaped swing.

Opening up in bunkers

Most good bunker players play the majority of their shots with an open clubface (fig. 64). This means that the club is given a greater effective loft, popping the ball out more softly. You may find that in opening the clubface, the ball tends to drift away to the right in flight. If you simply play the bunker splash shot from a square stance, but with an open clubface, the ball will almost always finish to the right of target. To compensate for this, the whole stance should be opened up, so that the line across the feet is aimed left of target and the direction of the swing is aimed left. In technical terms, this is an open stance and an out-to-in swing. However, this idea often confuses club players who imagine that the club has to be swung very much across themselves, producing unnecessary contortions. It simply means that the clubface is open so that the ball will tend to pop out to the right. All I do to allow for this is to aim to a new target perhaps 6 feet (1.8 m) left of the flag (figs. 77 to 80).

Fig. 77   Figs. 77–80 The clubface is laid open in bunker shots to produce extra
height. You must aim the whole stance and swing perhaps 6 feet
(1.8 m) left of the target; the ball will pop out on target

Fig. 78

Fig. 79

Fig. 80

Judging distance

If you are a relatively inexperienced club golfer you will be well-advised to learn to play a splash shot of reasonably set length and not to be concerned too much with the exact distance. If you can learn to play a shot of perhaps 10 yards (9 m), it will be reasonably adequate for every shot from just around the green, though, of course, as your confidence increases you can begin to work at varying the length of the shot. There are three ways in which you can vary the length of the bunker splash shot.

The first method is the one I suggest for the average club golfer. In this, the idea is that you vary the amount of sand which is splashed out. The more sand you take, the more the blow on the ball is cushioned and the shorter distance it travels. Conversely, the less sand you take, the farther the ball will go. To vary the length of the shot in this way you need to look at a spot farther away from or closer to the ball, as necessary, and concentrate on making the club enter the sand at this chosen spot. For the very short bunker shot, you may therefore have to look at a spot some 3 inches (76 mm) behind the ball and try to make the club enter the sand at that point. You must remember, however, that the idea is still to splash right *through* the sand, without chopping into it or losing speed prematurely.

The second method is one I would use to vary the length from perhaps 10 to 20 yards (9–18 m). To produce this range of distances, a fairly simple way is to alter the amount by which the clubface is opened or closed. The more the clubface is opened, the greater the effective loft of the club and so the more height the ball is given. On the other hand, if you play a conventional splash shot with a virtually square clubface, the ball will fly with slightly less height and so travel slightly farther. This technique is particularly useful in producing the longer splash shot where you want a little more distance than usual.

The last method is the one most professionals use. The good bunker player is usually able to vary the distance of bunker shots around the green with a considerable degree of accuracy. This is done by a combination of slowing down the swing and swinging shorter where necessary. In this way, the professional can usually successfully play very short, delicate bunker shots which are often the most intimidating for the club golfer. However, the method the tournament player uses requires a great deal of skill and accuracy and is not something for the average player to copy. The club golfer is best advised to concentrate on keeping a fairly full swing for all splash shots, varying the amount of sand taken, rather than trying to adapt the speed and length of the swing before she is ready for the more advanced stage. The key points for good, sound bunker shots are slowness, fullness of the swing and, most important, looking at the spot where you want the clubhead to enter the sand.

Left: Fig. 81; *right*: Fig. 82 ▶

The buried ball

Whenever the ball is sitting badly in the bunker, the ordinary splash shot method has to be adapted so that the clubhead is still able to get below the very bottom of the ball. If the ball is only very slightly below the surface of the sand, the shot is really executed in much the same way, except that you have to concentrate on a little more lift in the backswing with the arms, so that you get slightly deeper down in the throughswing.

However, when the ball is plugged in the sand, or if it sits down in a depression or footprint, the technique should be entirely different. In this case, you have to aim at forcing the ball out. To do this, the clubface should be

held squarely or even slightly closed at address, rather than open. The ball should then be back in the feet to perhaps the centre of the stance, with the hands slightly ahead of the ball. The weight is then concentrated on the left foot, with the eyes focused on a spot just behind the ball (fig. 81). As the backswing takes place, the club is lifted quite sharply with the hands, breaking the wrists immediately in the takeaway and keeping the weight on the left foot. The downswing is then purely a question of chopping down into the sand just behind the ball and forcing it out (fig. 82). As the club will almost stick in the sand, do not expect a follow-through. All you can really hope for in this kind of shot is to get the ball out somewhere onto the green or fairway as the case may be. The distance produced cannot be controlled very accurately.

Fig. 83

Fig. 84

Figs. 81–84 With a buried ball, the clubface is held square or even slightly closed, smashing down into the sand just behind the ball

Playing from hard sand

One of the most difficult shots from a bunker is where the sand is hard and compacted. In this case, the conventional splash shot is impossible, for there is really no sand to splash out. In this instance, you have to play a shot which is just like the little up-and-over pitch shot played from the fairway. You can play this either with the sand iron or with a pitching wedge. The choice depends on the suitability of your sand iron for pitching. If the club has a particularly large flange, so that the leading edge of the club sits well off the ground, it may be quite unsuitable. However, if it sits so that the whole sole of the club is virtually on the ground, it is probably an excellent club for pitching.

The essence of playing these shots well is to judge very accurately the depth of the contact, so that you just scrape the ground on which the ball sits. This is made slightly harder from a bare bunker than from a shot from bare ground in that you have to start with the clubhead above the sand at address. I would always approach a shot like this by walking into the bunker to see exactly what shot faces me, and then stepping outside the bunker to have two or three practice swings. This acts as a kind of dress rehearsal in which to develop the feel for the necessary depth of contact of the shot, concentrating above all on scraping the ground in the right place. On bare ground, the accuracy required leaves no room for error.

The shot is played by swinging the club back and through, keeping the left wrist very firm, but using the legs very freely to produce the movement in the rest of the body.

The downhill bunker shot

Probably the most difficult of all bunker shots is the one from a downhill lie, where the ball has just trickled into the back of the bunker. This is a shot which even the best professionals find testing. The reason is twofold. Firstly, on any downhill shot, the main problem is to be able to strike the ball without making contact with too much ground behind it. The second problem is that the downhill lie effectively acts to reduce the loft of the club being used. On a downhill lie, even the loft of a sand iron is reduced quite considerably. So, there are two problems – one of achieving a good contact and the other of producing good height to negotiate any obstacle in front.

In the set-up with this kind of shot, the most important fundamental is to set the body at right angles to the slope, so that the shoulders are parallel to the ground. If you position yourself correctly you can swing up and down the slope without catching the ground excessively somewhere behind the ball. In doing this, the weight must be pushed well onto the left foot to a point where you feel most uncomfortable and almost to be toppling away from the slope. Do not worry how awkward this feels. It will do. The ball is then played quite well back in the stance, towards the right foot, with the clubhead positioned a

Fig. 86

Fig. 85

Figs. 85–86 The downhill bunker shot: the ball is played back in the stance, and the shoulders follow the slope

couple of inches behind the ball, with the eyes focused on this spot (fig. 85). As the backswing takes place, the weight must be kept on the left foot, and you should concentrate on a really slow, controlled takeaway. In the downswing you must then concentrate on swinging the clubhead right *down* the slope beyond the ball, without any attempt to lift it. The lower you can keep the club beyond impact the better (fig. 87).

Fig. 87

Fig. 88

Figs. 87–88 Always hit *down* the slope. Never try to lift the ball

This is a difficult shot to execute and one in which you can never expect to produce much height, even with the sand iron. The ball will usually rise only 2 or 3 feet (61–91 cm), so that it is quite pointless to attempt to play from a downhill lie over a steep bank. It is a shot with definite limitations – so you must be relatively cautious and not attempt the impossible.

Fairway bunker shots

Whenever maximum length is required from a bunker, the technique is different once again. Ideally the ball should be struck as cleanly as possible, with the minimum amount of sand. There are two ways of playing the long bunker shot, which depend on the way in which the ball sits in the sand. If the ball sits completely on the top of the sand, the aim is to produce a slightly thin contact, without touching the sand at all. To make this as simple as possible, the eyes should be focused on the back of the ball, or even slightly towards the top of it. This helps you to hit the ball fractionally higher than normal, so that you avoid touching the sand. This type of shot is ideal when there is virtually no bank in front of the ball, so that the shot can be played with a long or medium iron, depending on the length of shot required or the height of any lip. Bear in mind that, if anything, the contact may be too thin, in which case the shot may go slightly lower than expected. You must therefore be careful to take a club with enough loft to negotiate any bank in front with some room to spare.

Whenever the ball sits slightly down in the sand, a different approach is required with the long bunker shot. In this case, it should be played in exactly the same way as you would tackle an ordinary fairway iron shot, where a divot is to be taken. The ball is ideally played from roughly the centre of the stance, hands fractionally ahead of the ball, and with the weight fairly evenly between the feet – if anything, favouring the left foot. The eyes are then focused on the back of the ball, and not the sand, and the thought in the swing should be to hit down and through the ball and then the sand – just the equivalent of taking a divot. As far as judging distances is concerned, if you play a shot from this kind of lie, the shot will probably fly some 10 yards (9 m) less than for the equivalent fairway shot. On the other hand, where the ball sits entirely on the top of the sand and you aim at producing a completely clean contact, there is likely to be no loss of distance and you might even produce a slightly longer shot than from grass.

12 Shotmaking and situation golf

It is impossible to become a really good golfer simply by standing on the practice ground and learning to hit full shots with the driver and irons. If you are to score well at golf – and that is, after all, the main aim of the game – you have to have a full repertoire of shots to fit the variety of situations you will encounter on a golf course. It would almost be possible to fill a whole book on the skills of playing situation golf, but the rest of this chapter is concerned with the most common problem shots which the golfer faces.

Recovering from thick rough

The major problem in recovering from thick rough is not so much one of executing the shot, as of deciding on the ideal route back to the fairway. The professional player will usually be relatively conservative in her choice of shot, playing back onto the fairway and being content with wasting a shot, rather than trying to pull off some miracle and thereby possibly wasting several more shots. For the longer-handicap player, the best rule is to take the shortest route back into play, unless the ball is obviously sitting well enough so that rather more distance can *safely* be achieved. It is too easy to be too ambitious with this kind of recovery shot in the hope that much more length can be made up than is possible. The sensible attitude is to play within your own capabilities and not to expect to pull off the perfect shot on every occasion.

As far as the execution of the shot is concerned, the choice of club is of paramount importance. The pitching wedge or 9-iron is probably the best choice, for both clubs have relatively heavy heads and are ideally suited to rip through the grass. Again – do not be too ambitious and try to take a 5-iron when the lie simply does not lend itself to this club. The grip on the club should be firm – certainly firmer than for the ordinary fairway shot. This will help you to hold on well through impact and so to keep the clubhead from turning as it meets the thick grass. The weight should be kept well on the left foot at address and also in the backswing, with the right shoulder riding rather higher than normal at address. This change helps to produce a slightly higher, steeper swing, which is one of the essentials of most recovery shots. Having produced a steep backswing, breaking the wrists early, the weight should be pushed back smartly onto the left foot, so that the ball is struck with a steep, downward contact. Do not be alarmed if the clubhead simply gets grabbed by the grass and does not continue through to a full finish. This kind of shot

129

largely requires brute force, combined with a steep swing, a firm grip and plenty of concentration on watching the ball really well through impact.

Chipping to a banked green

With any shot around the green where the ball has to go over some kind of bank, the club player instinctively seems to assume that it is best to play a high shot with a wedge, which would carry over the bank and land on the green. In fact, this is not usually the ideal shot, and the shot the club player usually attempts is far more difficult than is necessary. The simplest way of playing a ball up most banks is to run it up. Provided the bank is not too bumpy, and the grass is not too thick, it is often most sensible to take the putter and simply roll the ball up the slope. All you have to do is to concentrate on giving the ball enough speed to ensure that it really does get to the top of the bank.

If it is clearly not possible to putt the ball, because the grass is too thick or the ground is unpredictable, the next choice should be to think of running the ball up the bank with a 5- or 6-iron. This is played in much the same way as an ordinary chip from around the green, but with the addition that you should keep the hands slightly farther forward, so that the ball goes off a little lower. What one should be aiming at doing is just to set the ball moving through the air, but to get it down onto the ground again before it reaches the bottom of the slope. In this way, it will run smoothly up the bank, without being checked on bouncing. The distance is not particularly hard to judge, and all you really have to be concerned with is to give the ball enough speed to get it to the top of the bank.

The last choice I would make is to pitch the ball, and I would play this shot only if it is quite certain that neither the putt nor the running shot are suitable. The distance here is very much more critical; the shot is harder to execute and there is far more danger if the shot is not executed perfectly. This shot is particularly dangerous if the flag is close to the edge of the green, for you are often tempted to try to land the ball right at the top of the bank, with the result that a shot which is not perfect lands too short and rolls back down the slope. I would therefore use this shot only if the grass up the bank is too thick, or if the slope is very bumpy, or where there is plenty of green with which to work once the slope is negotiated. In executing this type of shot, be very certain to pick out the spot where you want the ball to land, walking up onto the green to get a true view of the green, and then, in the shot itself make your main rule to be that of watching the ball really well through impact, curbing any tendency to look up a moment too early.

Playing into a bank

In some cases, the best shot to play when negotiating a really steep bank around the green is to punch the ball straight into the bank and then let it jump on up. This is an ideal shot to play when the bank is very steep – perhaps 6 feet

(1.8 m) high – but not quite vertical, with the flag positioned just over the top. The pitch shot from such a position is often dangerous – you simply cannot hope to get close enough to the hole for a single putt without playing a very risky shot. On the other hand, if you are bold enough to punch the ball firmly at the bank it will simply pop straight up after it strikes the bank and land fairly softly on top without running forward much farther. The advantage of this shot is that the strength with which it is hit is not particularly crucial. If you hit it very hard, all that happens is that it pops up a little higher, but it will not travel far once it lands on the top. So, the technique is to use a 4- or 5-iron, hands well ahead of the ball, eyes firmly focused on the back of the ball and to punch it smartly into the bank.

Punching a ball low

Very frequently the club player finds herself behind and slightly beneath overhanging trees where it is necessary to punch the ball out with plenty of distance, but to keep it very low. This shot is an extension of the basic chipping and pitching technique. The shot can ideally be played with a 3- or 4-iron, setting-up to it in very much the same way as one would with a 50- or 60-yard (46–55 m) pitch. In other words, the hands should be kept well ahead of the ball and clubhead – thus reducing the effective loft of the club slightly – with the stance opened so that you are slightly facing the hole, to offset having the ball back in the stance. The shot is executed like a long pitch, taking the club back with a very early wrist break, and then punching it away with a short, firm finish. Once again, it is an unusual shot, where the two halves of the swing do not mirror one another. You use the hands on the backswing but then look for a very solid, punchy finish.

Before executing this shot it is always wise to have a couple of practice swings to ensure that the club is going to be able to move without being obstructed by trees above or in front of you.

This type of shot is also useful, in a slightly modified form, when playing on seaside courses or in other conditions when you want a shot which flies low into the green. It can be played in just the same way, with any club from the 3-iron to pitching wedge, simply by moving the hands farther ahead of the ball to reduce the effective loft, opening the stance to compensate for the ball being farther back in the feet and then concentrating on an early wrist break in the backswing, but short, solid follow-through.

Producing extra height

When extra height is required from a grassy lie on the fairway or in light rough, the technique is to give the ball an extra flick of the wrist through impact, as though almost trying to whip it up into the air. The movement is very sudden – a kind of throwing action in which you add extra backspin to the shot. However, this is possible only if there is plenty of grass under the ball, so that you can be sure of striking the very bottom of the ball.

When the lie is not so good, the problem of achieving extra height is slightly greater. Added height is produced as a rule by opening the clubface, so that the effective loft of the club is increased. However, whenever this is done, the effect is the same as you get with the open faced wedge, for the ball tends to drift away to the right. The simple remedy is that whenever extra height is needed, and the clubface is opened, you should compensate for this by aiming to a mental target to the left of the real target.

Playing from sidehill lies

The majority of golfers learn to play golf on fairly flat practice areas or driving ranges, after which they find varying degrees of difficulty in playing shots from sloping lies. The shot in which a player stands below the ball is usually the easier of the two sidehill lies for the club golfer. This is because it minimises the usual tendency to slice. In this shot, the feet are very much below the ball, so that the ball is now somewhere opposite the knees. This means that, as you stand to the ball, the posture is automatically more erect, with the ball farther from the feet than it would normally be. Any awkward feeling might be helped by holding the club several inches down the shaft. When you stand in this way it means that the club is likely to swing more around the body than is normal on a flatter plane (fig. 89). This different plane of swing has the effect of tending to produce a shot which hooks away to the left. You need think of very little by way of special technique in this shot, other than to maintain balance especially well and to aim away to the right to allow for the likely hook. The ball will not only bend quite considerably from right to left in the air, but it is also likely to land on ground which also slopes this same way. You should therefore aim well to the right – probably much more than the club golfer imagines – and be prepared for the shot to hook away to the left.

In standing above the ball, the problems are the reverse and this is usually a relatively difficult shot for the average golfer. In this position you have to bend over considerably more to the ball, bringing it much closer to the feet. With the body in this stooped posture, the plane of the swing tends to be more upright than normal and the major problem is to stay down sufficiently through impact to produce a solid contact. You have to have the feeling of almost bending *down* into the shot before and through impact and resist any tendency to look away from the ball too early. With this steeper plane of swing, the ball will almost always slice away to the right in flight, kicking farther right on landing. Therefore, aim quite considerably to the left of target – usually very much more than you might expect (fig. 90).

The main point to remember about these shots is the way the ball is likely to curve in the air; the execution of the shot is not so difficult except from a really steep slope. The simple way to remember which way the ball will bend is that it will always curve in the air in the same direction as it would roll on the ground. In other words, with the ball *above* your feet, it will tend to run towards you; it will also curve towards you in flight – that is, a hook. With the ball below your feet, it will tend to run away from you down the slope; it will also curve away from you in flight – a slice.

Fig. 89 In standing below the ball, aim right to allow for a hook

Fig. 90 In standing above the ball, aim left to allow for a slice

Figs. 91–92 The downhill shot: weight left, shoulders following the slope

A long downhill shot

The downhill shot is not generally easy. There are two problems. Firstly, you have to be able to achieve a contact which is clean, without scuffing the ground before the ball. Secondly, with the club positioned on a down slope, the effective loft of the club is reduced if you take up the correct address position. It is therefore much more difficult to produce sufficient height.

The correct set-up is all important for this shot. The basic principle is to stand with the weight well on the left foot, setting the body at right angles to the slope so that the shoulders follow the line of the ground. In this way, you can swing up and down the slope in much the same way as you would swing relative to horizontal ground (fig. 91). The ball is positioned well towards the right foot, hands ahead of the ball, and it is this ball placement which has the effect of reducing the effective loft of the club. The 6-iron will now hit a shot with the trajectory of, perhaps, a 3-iron while the long irons and fairway woods have the loft reduced to such an extent that they are often virtually impossible to play from downhill lies.

In executing the shot the main emphasis must be on keeping the weight well towards the left foot, so that the correct downward attack is encouraged. Through impact you must have a definite feeling of staying down with the shot, of trying to keep the clubhead following the slope of the ground for several inches after striking the ball, and of resisting any tendency to come up too early.

In playing the downhill shot, there is nearly always a tendency for the ball to fade away to the right in flight. Allow for this by aiming the whole stance and shot to an imaginary target well left of the flag.

A short, downhill pitch

A particularly unpleasant shot to have to play is one from a steep downhill bank, where the ball has to be pitched over some obstacle in front. The problems are very much the same as for the longer downhill shot – both in producing a clean contact and in producing sufficient height. It is essential to use either a sand iron or a pitching wedge to get much height at all. Weight must be pushed as much onto the left foot as possible, so that the right shoulder is well up at address. All of this will, and should, feel awkward. The next step is to have a couple of practice swings of the takeaway and backswing to ensure that you can get the club up and down very steeply, without scuffing the ground behind the ball. The more you can keep the weight on the left foot, and the higher the right shoulder is set, the steeper the takeaway can be. In executing the shot the two most important points are to watch the ball really well through impact and to ensure that the clubhead is kept travelling right *down* the slope beyond impact.

Playing from an uphill lie

Uphill shots are generally much easier than downhill shots, for the uphill lie produces maximum height and eliminates any tendency to slice. There are two distinct ways of playing from this type of slope. With a long iron or wood the better method is to set the body out at right angles from the slope, so that the weight is back on the right foot very slightly, with the line of the shoulders following the slope of the ground. The ball can then be fairly well forward in the stance, towards the left foot, so that the loft of the club is increased – helping to produce plenty of height. The tendency in this shot is for the ball to pull away to the left in flight so that one simply aims away to the right, taking an extra club to allow for the added height. The swing is basically as for any other fairway shot except that a determined effort must be made to push the

Fig. 93 A short uphill shot, leaning *into* the slope at address

weight well onto the left foot through impact. The steeper the slope, the more difficult this is.

The other approach to this kind of shot is quite different and is probably more suited to playing medium and short irons, or for short shots from a steep bank. In this case, the weight is set well towards the left foot, so that you are leaning *into* the bank, with the left leg as bent as necessary to keep the body upright (fig. 93). Your weight is then kept well on the left foot throughout the swing, the aim at impact being to punch the club into the slope, taking a solid divot and forcing the ball away. A strong player can use this method for long iron shots, but for the club player it is probably limited to the shorter irons. With this method, very little difference in flight is produced from an ordinary shot, though there may be a tendency to push the ball slightly right of target if you lean too much onto the left foot through impact.

Playing into the wind

The main rule to remember in playing into a wind is *not* to try to hit the ball harder than usual and not to try to fight the wind. If anything, you should swing more easily; simply take more club to allow for the wind and concentrate above all else on balancing really well through impact and in the follow-through. A danger in playing in the wind is that the swing becomes faster and faster and you try to hit the ball with far too much force. Instead, you should take two or three clubs more than usual and work at a really smooth swing. When a ball is hit into a headwind it will usually take up height more easily than normal, so that a player should never be afraid of hitting a long iron or fairway wood into the wind. The downfall of most club players is that they simply do not take enough club and so force their shots and lose balance.

For many players, the most difficult shot to play into a headwind is the drive. Any tendency to hit the ball too high is exaggerated. The usual problem of the player who produces drives which are too high is that, in thinking of trying to keep the ball down, she starts to strike the ball with a downward contact instead of with the correct upward one. The more you hit *down* into the ball with a driver, the higher it flies. The bottom of the swing with a drive must be some eight inches *behind* the ball and not right behind or beneath it. The professional golfer can very often produce a slightly lower flight than normal simply by teeing the ball a fraction lower than usual. However, this is definitely not the method I would suggest for the player who tends to hit slightly skied drives. If you do this it will encourage you to hit even more down into the ball instead of producing the correct, shallow contact. The way to produce a suitable height of drive is to tee the ball up as normal but to concentrate with great determination on taking the ball from the top of the tee and so leaving the tee in the ground. In that way, you aim to take, perhaps, the top 95 per cent of the ball, so that the backspin is reduced very slightly.

Playing the tee shots

Tee shots, either with the driver or on par-3 holes, should really be the easiest shots to play. After all, you can choose the exact spot from which to play the ball, tee up to the desired height and tread down the ground around the ball if necessary. To make tee shots as easy as possible take great care in deciding where to tee the ball. Firstly, choose an absolutely flat stance, going back behind the tee box, up to the permitted two clublengths, if necessary. Then, more importantly, consider which side of the tee gives the easier shot and do not simply tee up at the closest point to where you happen to be standing. On a wide tee, the shot from one side may look entirely different from the shot from the other. If you tee up well towards the right of the tee, you are then automatically aiming slightly across the fairway towards the left side and so away from any trouble on the right. On the other hand, if you set-up towards the left of the tee, you turn away from trouble down the left side, and slightly towards the right side of the hole. This type of choice may be wise if trouble lies down one side of the fairway and you want to be turned slightly away from it or if you feel more comfortable on one side of the tee than the other. This choice can also change the appearance of a shot to a par-3 hole quite dramatically.

Whenever you play a tee shot with a club other than a driver, the height of the tee can be quite crucial. The majority of longer-handicap players tend to tee the ball much too high with iron shots from a tee, and also in playing a shot with a 3- or 4-wood. All that is necessary is to tee the ball up sufficiently high so that you have the equivalent of playing from a very good lie on the fairway. The tee should therefore be pushed down so that only its head is above ground, or with perhaps a quarter of an inch of the neck showing for a 3- or 4-wood shot. If the ball is teed too high you may well go underneath the ball with the woods and produce excessive height, or catch the ball from the top half of the blade of the iron where there is really no power.

Deciding when to gamble

Many golfers waste shots around the course, not because of badly executed shots but because of taking wrong decisions. Whenever you are faced with a recovery situation, it is really necessary to ask yourself where you hope to put the ball and what you will try to achieve with the next shot. Players often take an unnecessary gamble at producing extra length, or carrying over a cross-bunker, when nothing is really achieved if the shot is successful but much may be lost if it is less than perfect. In this kind of situation, it is absolutely essential to plan the next two or three shots. It is quite pointless, for example, trying to force extra length out of a shot from the rough, if it is going to be risky and still leave you a wedge shot to the green. There may be a perfectly safe shot out onto the fairway which would then leave an 8- or 9-iron to the flag. On the other hand, you are often faced with a ditch or cross-bunkers to carry where the gamble is simply not worth taking. If you play the safe shot short, it may only leave 100 yards (91m) to the green. If you attempt the carry, you may still be left with an awkward little shot of 50 or 60 yards (45 or 55m). By all means, if you can actually get onto the green and so possibly stand to save a shot, take the gamble – it might be worthwhile. But, really, it is worth gambling only if you stand to achieve something which is worth the risk. Of course, you can, and do, make a wrong decision at times, but the point is that you should at least weigh up the risks and rewards before attempting shots which clearly flirt with danger.

Short pitching from the rough

A little shot which can often be much more difficult than you imagine is the really short pitch from light, fluffy rough. The problem lies in the fact that the speed of the swing has to be so slow that the grass grabs the clubhead through impact, speed is lost and the ball drops several feet, or even yards, short of the target. As with most short shots, a few practice swings can be very helpful in producing the necessary feel of the shot. The major change to make in these circumstances is to ensure that you keep a very firm grip and emphasise the feeling of swinging the clubhead through the ball to a definite follow-through position of the same length as the backswing. This helps to ensure that the clubhead is kept moving right through impact, so that speed is not lost.

13 Ten keys to better golf

Swinging through the ball

In every full shot in golf, it is essential to have the feeling of swinging right *through* the ball and not at the ball. The professional player always produces a really long, full follow-through in the drive, in which the club usually hits her somewhere around the left shoulder blade at the finish of the swing. Thinking of this keeps her accelerating through impact. By contrast, the club golfer usually hits *at* the ball, pulling up with a short, incomplete finish so that speed is lost by impact. To produce maximum speed, work at the fullest follow-through possible with the long shots, ensuring that the club shaft makes contact with the left shoulder or back in the finish.

Balance – the key to consistency

Players are often told that they are guilty of trying to hit the ball too hard or of swinging too fast. The root of the trouble here is usually not so much the speed being produced – after all, we all want maximum clubhead speed – but that players lose balance through and beyond impact. Nearly every really good player produces perfect poise and balance in the follow-through, which in turn means that she has been perfectly balanced through impact. Balance through impact is vital, for it helps to keep the clubhead swinging through in the intended path. Any tendency to fall forward will bring the clubhead too far from the feet at impact; falling back to the right tends to bring the clubhead down into the ground too soon. Balance is vital. What I would therefore advise every player, of whatever standard, to work at is to hold a perfectly poised follow-through at the end of every shot. When playing on the course, hold the balance on *every* shot for a count of three seconds, regardless of where the ball has gone. Concentrate on making the swing *look* really good and imagine someone is always there to take a photograph of the finish. If you work at this, the bad shots will gradually disappear and your game will develop greater consistency.

Visualising every shot

It is essential in every golf shot to have a positive image of the flight of the ball required. For long shots, the top-class golfer will usually produce a bad shot only if she is unable to get the right image in her mind. The image which she produces is like a visual instruction to her brain and body, so that if she can imagine the ball flying high and straight she has very much more chance of hitting the right shot than if all she can imagine is the ball hooking away out of bounds. For this reason, you must never allow yourself to have a negative image of what is *not* required. This is disastrous. If you see a picture of the ball slicing, that is what it will tend to do.

This visualisation is of paramount importance in the short game too. You should not only pick out the right spot on which to land the ball with pitch shots, but you should also be able to have a very strong image of the desired flight of the ball. If you allow yourself to 'see' the ball being fluffed short into a bunker, or being thinned through the green, your brain unfortunately takes this as its instruction and does its best to produce just the shot you *do not* want!

Think of the contact with the ball

The accuracy required in the contact between club and ball is really rather alarming when you think about it. After all, the club is being swung up through an arc of some 12 feet (4 m) and down to the ball again at maximum speed, with the aim of brushing the ground at an exact spot beneath the ball about half an inch (13 mm) in diameter. The inexperienced golfer, and even the average player, is usually unable to produce this tremendous accuracy of contact on every shot. What you have to realise is that the bad shot at golf is not necessarily produced by a bad swing. A very good-looking swing, which may be half an inch (13 mm) out at impact, can have disastrous results. To improve at golf and eliminate bad shots does not always require a change in the swing, but may simply be a question of learning to produce greater accuracy at impact. A good golfswing and accuracy at contact do not necessarily go together. The beginner will usually bring the club down anywhere within an area perhaps 3 inches by 3 inches (76 × 76 mm) and varying in depth by an inch or so. However good the swing looks, this is simply not accurate enough to make a decent contact on the majority of shots. The average club golfer will usually bring the clubhead down within an area an inch (25 mm) in diameter, so that the vast majority of her shots are contacted well, but there is likely to be an occasional shot which is caught slightly off-centre.

Let me emphasise that, having developed a golfswing of whatever kind, you *must* work at producing greater accuracy of contact, simply by thinking about the desired contact. It will not just happen. By the same reasoning, a bad shot at golf is not necessarily caused by a bad swing but may simply be a question of some small error in the contact.

Relaxation

If you are to produce maximum clubhead speed through impact, the hands and wrists must perform what amounts to a throwing action through the ball. In order to be able to do this, the arms and wrists must be relatively loose and relaxed. As a general rule, the stiffer and more tense you are, the less able the hands are to work and the more likely the ball is to be sliced away to the right. The player who is almost too loose and relaxed is more likely to be prone to hooking. For this reason, the tournament professional may stress firmness in the swing, but do bear in mind that her problem is far more likely to be one of hooking, while the club golfer errs, as a rule, on the side of slicing.

The other kind of tension is that of literally trying too hard. The more you key yourself up for the important shot, the more tense you are likely to become, and the worse the result. There are two kinds of golfers, and you have to know which kind of player you are and adjust your game accordingly. There are those players who need a certain amount of competitive tension and literally thrive on being *slightly* tense and keyed up. This kind of player needs to will the ball into the hole and the harder she tries, the better she performs. On the other hand, the other kind of golfer seizes up under tension and needs to develop a 'couldn't care less attitude' about the game. For her, the need is to take tension off herself and to keep on saying to herself, 'It doesn't really matter what happens'. Find out which kind of player you are and then train yourself either to urge yourself on, or to adopt a relaxed attitude, as is necessary.

Hit every shot for itself

Although there has to be some planning of shots at many holes, it is absolutely essential to take each shot as an individual task when actually executing it. Always try to forget what has gone before and simply concentrate on hitting every shot to the best of your ability, without worrying about the score. If you can learn to string together shot after shot, good scores just begin to happen. If the holes before have been disastrous, do not try to make up ground. You cannot do better than your best – and you should be attempting to play every shot to the best of your ability. So, once again, it is a question of not trying too hard, but of persevering, hitting shot after shot and waiting to see what happens.

Think of speed, not force

In order to produce maximum length to your shots, the key factor is to develop maximum speed *in the clubhead*. What you do not want is force in the body. If you attempt to force the shot, the muscles of the wrists and hands tighten up and speed is in fact lost. It is very, very tempting to try to hit the ball too hard but that means you are developing force instead of speed.

Whenever extra length is your aim, bear in mind that you cannot produce more length than is normal to your game, except if a little added speed can be produced with an extra flick of the wrists through impact.

The swing as two movements

When my pupils have difficulty with the swing, I suggest that they return to the basic concept of the swing. This helps to clear the mind of unwanted theory and enables them to start afresh. The aim of the golfswing is very simply to swing the *clubhead* up into a position at the top of the backswing, from which you want to swing it right on through in a circle which brushes the ground at the spot where the ball is. To achieve this most efficiently, the body performs two co-ordinated movements. The body turns to the right and then through to the left again, while the arms swing up and down and up again. In other words, you turn to the right and lift the club with the arms, and then turn on through, while the arms swish the club through and then lift in the finish of the swing. The better you time the two together, the better the overall swing will be. One of the keys to a good golfswing, which lasts from year to year with only small, minor adjustments, is to keep a simple concept of the whole thing. It is not a series of positions and separate movements, but a full, flowing *swing*. I think, therefore, it is always worth asking yourself, when you have a real problem, 'Could what I am doing really be described as a *swing*?' Allow the club to move freely, simplify the ideas of what you are trying to do and return to basics – a turn of the body and a lift of the arms.

Watching the ball through impact

Perhaps the most important thing of all in the swing, whatever else you do, is to concentrate on watching the ball. This is absolutely fundamental for everything from putting to driving. There should be a split second in which you are conscious of the ball having gone and that you are left looking down at the ground beneath. With the long shots, unless you are very supple in the neck, it may be necessary to bring the eyes and head on up almost the moment the ball is struck, but you *must* be aware of seeing the ball at impact. The professional golfer will usually keep her head absolutely still until the very end of the swing, without inhibiting the length and fullness of the follow-through. The club player has to achieve the happy medium, watching the ball through impact, but allowing herself to go right on through to a full finish.

With short shots it is equally vital to watch the ball well. There is no question of losing the ball, so you should concentrate on keeping the eyes down for a good two seconds after impact. A little exaggeration does no harm here; it simply gives you some margin for error if you are tempted to look up slightly early when under pressure. Looking at the ball, and keeping your eye on it, eliminates the truly bad shots of golf.

Back to basics

My last advice, to golfers of all standards, is – if in doubt about your game, return to the very basics. The vast majority of faults have their source in the grip and the set-up. At the first sign of trouble look at these before anything else. A good player, or average player, is likely to produce a real change in her swing only if, in some way, she is set-up differently. The set-up needs constant checking and will change almost week by week by small but critical amounts. The true basics of a good golfswing are the grip, stance, watching the ball through impact and, perhaps most important, perfect balance. With these under control you can concentrate on the main aim of the game, simply developing the ability to produce better scores.

Index

aiming 35, 37, 79–80, 85, 98

backspin 9
backswing 28, 42–52, 80, 142
balance 64, 137, 139
ball position
  bunker shots 114–28
  long shots 31, 71, 79, 80
  short shots 31, 111
  sloping lies 132–6
bunker shot 114–28
buried ball 123–4

chipping 100–4, 130
closed stance 85
clubface
  closed 21, 24, 69, 81, 83
  open 24, 86, 110, 117
  square 9, 96
concentration 6, 37, 71
contact 31, 70–1, 73, 89–91,
  104, 125, 137, 140
cut shots 131–2

direction 31, 43, 52
distance from the ball 28, 35,
  89
downhill lie 125, 127, 134–5
driving 24, 71–5, 86, 137–8

elbow 62–4, 86

fairway woods 24, 70–1, 135
feel 76–7, 99, 104, 112
follow-through 64, 83, 139, 142

grip
  hooker's 24, 81
  interlocking 21
  overlapping 16
  putting 94
  size of 27
  strong 24, 81
  Vardon 16, 21, 94
  weak 24, 86

hand action 49–51, 69, 86, 113
height of tee 75
high shot 69, 131–2, 137
hook 9, 21, 24, 27, 81, 83, 85,
  86, 132

imagery 108, 140
impact 13, 65, 69, 70, 89, 111,
  143
inside attack 52

judgement 76–7, 98–9, 104,
  112

knee 28, 32–3, 35, 49

left arm 42–51, 60–4, 83, 86,
  101
left hand 14, 16, 19, 21, 24, 46,
  50, 60–4, 83
left heel 49, 53
long iron 24, 27, 69–70, 135
long putting 99
low shot 21, 131

mental approach 38–9, 70, 108,
  114, 138, 140

Niklaus, Jack 6, 7, 21

par 3's 137
pitching 100–13, 138
plane 43, 47, 48, 132
posture 32–7
practice swing 12, 31, 92, 93
psychology 38, 70, 108, 114,
  138, 140
putting 94–9

reading the green 98
recovery shot 27, 129–38
relaxation 27, 61, 69, 86, 89,
  93, 117, 141
rough 129, 138

sand iron 107, 110, 114, 127,
  135
shank 90–1
short iron 31, 65
shoulder 28, 30, 35, 37, 43, 47,
  63, 64, 71
sidehill lie 86–91, 132–3
sidespin 12, 81–91
simplicity 38, 39
skied drive 75, 93, 137
slicing 12, 24, 27, 37, 62, 77,
  132–3
squareness 35, 37, 96
stance
  irons 28
  bunker 114
  driving 71, 75
  open 68, 111, 114, 117
  putting 95–6
straight left arm 30

takeaway 52, 73, 135
target 79
tee shot 71–5, 137–8
tension 27, 61, 69, 86, 93, 98,
  141
thumb 14, 16, 21, 24, 39, 94
timing 6, 39, 64, 69, 71
topped shot 93
turn and lift 39, 43, 47–8, 52,
  53, 142

uphill lie 135–6

watching the ball 92, 93, 98,
  108, 112, 143
weight transference 49, 53, 81,
  93, 111, 135, 136
width of stance 28
wind play 136–7
wrist action 24, 49–51, 69, 86,
  113